URBAN
faery
MAGICK

ABOUT THE AUTHOR

Tara Sanchez has been practicing her craft as a Druid Sorceress for nearly twenty years. She is a Gardnerian High Priestess, a member of the Order of Bards, Ovates & Druids, and a card-slinging faery botherer. Tara lives in Cheshire, UK, with her husband and faithful hound, and she spends her time writing, teaching workshops, running a training coven, speaking at moots and conferences, and reading the cards. Contact information for the author can be found at www.tarasanchez.com.

URBAN
ꝼaery
MAGICK

CONNECTING
TO THE FAE IN THE
MODERN WORLD

TARA SANCHEZ

Llewellyn Publications
Woodbury, Minnesota

FIRST EDITION
First Printing, 2021

Cover design by Shannon McKuhen
Cover illustration by Ken McCuen
Interior photos © Tara Sanchez

Llewellyn Publications is a registered trademark of Llewellyn Worldwide Ltd.

Library of Congress Cataloging-in-Publication Data
Names: Sanchez, Tara, author.
Title: Urban faery magick : connecting to the fae in the modern world /
  Tara Sanchez.
Description: First edition. | Woodbury, Minnesota : Llewellyn Publications,
  2021. | Includes bibliographical references and index.
Identifiers: LCCN 2020051557 (print) | LCCN 2020051558 (ebook) | ISBN
  9780738764214 (paperback) | ISBN 9780738764368 (ebook)
Subjects: LCSH: Fairies. | Magic. | Cities and towns—Folklore.
Classification: LCC BF1552 .S26 2021 (print) | LCC BF1552 (ebook) | DDC
  133.9—dc23
LC record available at https://lccn.loc.gov/2020051557
LC ebook record available at https://lccn.loc.gov/2020051558

Llewellyn Worldwide Ltd. does not participate in, endorse, or have any authority or responsibility concerning private business transactions between our authors and the public.

All mail addressed to the author is forwarded but the publisher cannot, unless specifically instructed by the author, give out an address or phone number.

Any internet references contained in this work are current at publication time, but the publisher cannot guarantee that a specific location will continue to be maintained. Please refer to the publisher's website for links to authors' websites and other sources.

Llewellyn Publications
A Division of Llewellyn Worldwide Ltd.
2143 Wooddale Drive
Woodbury, MN 55125-2989
www.llewellyn.com

Printed in the United States of America

OTHER BOOKS BY TARA SANCHEZ

*The Temple of Hekate: Exploring the Goddess Hekate Through Ritual,
Meditation and Divination* (Avalonia, 2011)

ACKNOWLEDGMENTS

This book was a long time in the making. I started drafting extended notes in 2006 at the encouragement of two great magickal friends; we had not long returned from an amazing retreat in Ireland, and it was becoming increasingly obvious that the Fae of the urban realms had something to say. They believed that I was to be one to speak for them, and I will always be eternally grateful to them for instilling that first spark of an idea into my mind. Despite the idea sitting on the back burner for over a decade, many people along the way made sure that I never forgot it was a book that should be written.

My long-suffering husbeast, Colin, who brings me food and reminds me when my coffee has gone cold, I would starve without you. My beautiful daughter, Jadzia—who has more than a little bit of the Fae about her—you, my darling girl, have always reminded me when I need to go and dance with the faeries. To Kristoffer, who nagged me into taking a chance and submitting a proposal when the opportunity came up, thanks for having faith in me. To Paolo Di, who helped me with the *Aradia* translations, you are a truly inspiring and magickal person. I hope we can do another project again soon. To George, who dared to share. To David Rankine, who always kindly points me in the direction of the right grimoire when I ask, thank you, my friend; my practice would be a lot less without you.

I thank the Mother for her blessings and the help that I have received.
I offer this book as a sign of my respect.

CONTENTS

EXERCISES AND MEDITATIONS

Chapter 9

Chapter 10

Chapter 11

Chapter 12

Chapter 13

Chapter 14

introduction

I believe in fairies, the myths, dragons.
It all exists, even if it's in your mind.
Who's to say that dreams and nightmares
aren't as real as the here and now?[1]

Humanity has always believed in something other. Our folkloric stories are full of nymphs and pixies, elves and goblins. In some parts of the world even today, belief in the supernatural is so strong that the course of roads has been changed and buildings resited in an attempt to appease or, better still, avoid supernatural wrath altogether. Despite our best endeavors to ignore them, we are both drawn to and repulsed by these creatures.

I remember being told as a child by the older children that faeries lived in the hedgerow that surrounded the local playground. If you went there at midnight on a moonlit night and circled the swings skipping backward, the faeries would come out and play with you. Enthralled by such a wondrous and exciting concept, I harassed every child in the street, badgering them until they agreed that we would go together and see if the stories were true. On the chosen night, I stood at my window, staring at the moonbeams and shivering in anticipation, convinced that every shadow moved with creatures from the otherworld. The clock ticked as I waited for the older children to emerge from their homes and give me the signal that we were ready. But no child ever appeared. Midnight grew ever closer and eventually ticked away.

The following day, I challenged the children about their nonappearance only to be told that they had, in fact, gone to the playground, and that they had

---

1. Attributed to John Lennon.

waited for me for as long as they could, but that I must have fallen asleep. Not true! Not true! I felt cheated and foolish. I knew I hadn't fallen asleep. The children were making fun of me; faeries weren't real. I quietly let the incident pass and resolved never to accept anything those children ever told me again. But I never quite stopped believing, and night after night I lay in my bed, restless, yearning to know if the faeries were dancing. Eventually, unable to take it any longer, I crept from my bed, dashing out of the house as fast as my tiny little legs would carry me. I remember making it to the playground, and I remember skipping around the swings, but after that, my next memory is of creeping back into bed. That night, my dreams were filled with color and light and dancing. Whether the faeries really came out to play with me, well, I leave that to your own judgment, but I like to believe that they did.

Regardless of the actual truth of the matter, that formative experience shaped and molded my belief system. As a teen and young adult, my reading material was folklore and fantasy fiction. Stories of elves and men and magick rings, gods who fell to earth as pieces of jade, and Druids with power over dragons who could make a king, and break him. At night, my wallpaper came alive with creatures that crawled from it, and voices whispered in the dark to me. It never occurred to me that these occurrences, these nighttime visitations, were anything other than real. Well into the latter half of my teens—before the indoctrination of society took over, affecting me enough to reject the fantastical world within—I coexisted with the creatures of myth and legend.

But, in truth, I never really stopped believing; I just didn't talk about it. Country walks would lead me down routes where I thought I could hear flutes playing, to places where the hairs on the back of my neck would stand up. Places where I would see great bulbous watery eyes staring back at me in the stillness at the edge of the millpond. Nighttime, too, would often leave me wracked with terror, and yet I had no explanation as to why. In a bid to understand this part of me, this uncomfortable "hole" in my psyche, I dabbled with evangelical spirituality during my early twenties. I spent a long time quite literally trying to pray the Fae away. Not an uncommon reaction to the shadow world that exists parallel to our own—people do it every day. Our folklore is full of stories of good Christian folk praying to God and the saints to cure them of a faery problem. Folklore is also full of thwarted attempts; it's hard to outwit the fair folk.

In the following pages, I will share what I have learned in the years since I finally accepted that faeries did indeed live at the bottom of my garden in the hopes that this information will help others along their path. I'd like to show that not all little children stop believing in faeries; some of us grow up choosing to dance with them.

WHO COULD BENEFIT FROM READING THIS BOOK?

Well, everybody of course, silly! In all seriousness though, of course I think that everyone should read my book. If you have picked this book up and made it past the blurb on the back cover, then the likelihood is that this book is for you. However, just to be on the safe side, I better make it clear that this book is not a book of fairy tales in the conventional sense.

If you have a desire to learn more about the Fae and how we coexist with them in an increasingly urban and modern world, then read on. Understand also that this is not specifically a book about nature spirits. Many of the denizens of the other realms are finding that when they cross into our space and time, the world they last visited has changed. Their habitats are no longer green and pleasant places, so some spirits fade from consciousness, choosing to retreat further into their own realms. But others are adapting, growing, and evolving—in some cases, positively thriving—in an increasingly broken landscape. These are the faeries we need to learn from.

This book is also aimed at those who struggle to relate when told they must find countryside and trees and rivers and hills in order to connect with the Fae. Perhaps they are unable to find or travel to these places, or maybe they are genuinely more comfortable in an urban environment.

Maybe you can connect to nature spirits in their natural environments already, but you can also sense something as you walk along that deserted street in the early morning, and you are curious to find out more. This book shall hopefully illustrate to you that the creatures of Faerie can be found in the most unlikely of places and in the strangest of forms. I will also demonstrate that, more often than not, faeries do not appear in the standard elemental forms they are usually categorized in, which is why they might go unnoticed. Finally, I hope to show that with some creative thought or by adapting traditional practices, you can interact with the other in town as easily as in the country. Whatever your reasons. I do hope you find what you are looking for.

—Cheshire, 2019

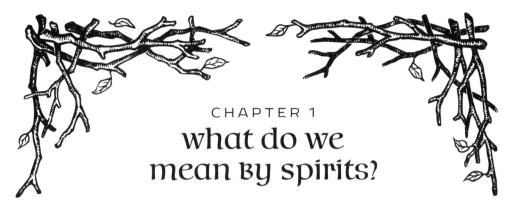

what do we mean by spirits?

Sarah: Ow! It bit me!
Hoggle: What'd you expect fairies to do?
Sarah: I thought they did nice things, like … like granting wishes.
Hoggle: Shows what *you* know, don't it?[2]

Before we get started in earnest, it is probably a good idea to discuss terminology. When discussing general subjects, I have chosen to use the terms *spirit*, *spirits of place*, *the Fae*, *fair folk*, and *faery* interchangeably. This is because these terms are already embedded within our human psyche. This is not to say that these spirits do not have other names—many of them do, and, as we will see later, many of these entities hold great store in the giving and receiving of names.

Some of these creatures we will explore could also be called *genius loci*, as they are the spirits of place, whatever that place may be. They aren't angels, demons, or ghosts, and they aren't some form of magnetic memory from another time. They are often fully sentient, although their understanding of our world and ethics can be a little strange and downright dangerous at times.

Feral is another term that will crop up here and there. It was a concept first taught to me a number of years ago by two very talented magicians, each an expert in their own fields, who have, as a result of their own "great works," spent time studying and interacting with the spirits of the natural world. My own path and perspective are different from theirs. But if they hadn't introduced me to the idea of a world of urban magick, this book would not exist.

---

2. Jim Henson, *Labyrinth* (UK: TriStar Pictures, 1986), film, 101 min.

Traditionally, a feral creature is one who was once domesticated, such as a cat or dog, and has returned to live in the wild or on city streets. Feral spirits are a little different. They are natural spirits who have found the boundary between the rural and urban realms considerably smaller than it once was. Many are in the process of adapting and evolving, and as part of this adaptation, they are consciously choosing to inhabit another world—the urban world that they find themselves in, leaving behind the sacred landscapes they once inhabited.

Dwellers in our human landscape are not actually a new phenomenon. Our folklore is riddled with stories of changeling children who are there because parents forgot to cross the poker irons across the cradle before their own offspring was baptized. Or of the house brownie who took great delight in spoiling the milk because their "services" were not appreciated by the humans who shared the house with them. However, the type and nature of these spirits were quite specific, and their roles were quite limited. As we expand and grow and change the world around us, so must the type and function of the entities with whom we coexist. So, it is not really surprising that it is increasingly as likely to find a wider spectrum of the fair folk on a city street as it is to find them on a lonely moor.

Whether this state of affairs is right or wrong is not a subject I am choosing to debate. I know some feel very strongly that the Fae should only be approached within a natural setting and anything else is wrong. They believe that, as walkers in the otherworlds, we should be strengthening the natural places of power, giving our energy to those who remain on the hill and field and in the lake and sea. And I have no great argument against that. But I also accept that there is more to this world. Some of us feel drawn to other, less rural places of power, and it is our path to strengthen those places when no one else will.

Things change slower for the genius loci. But change they do. As such, I chose to work with those who wish to show themselves to me, wherever and whenever they present themselves. Who are we to decide that one spirit or place is more worthy of our notice and energy than another?

A FEW CAUTIONARY WORDS

I love the scene in *Labyrinth* at the beginning of this chapter; I love it so much that I have quoted it a hundred or more times in talks I have given on this subject. I suspect that I will quote it hundreds of times more over my lifetime. If there is only one lesson that I manage to impart to readers of this book, I want this to be the one: the Fae can bite!

First, they do not understand our morals and ethics. Their problem-solving skills can be quite literal; if you ask the spirits of place to help you reduce the pollution along a riverbank, their solution may be to just remove the cause of the pollution. You may suddenly hear of a spate of drownings or of children and dogs slipping where previously they had never slipped before. Be very careful what you wish for when interacting with the Fae.

Despite the possible risks and pitfalls, walking with one foot in their realm can be very rewarding. If you choose to interact with the Fae, your own outlook and understanding of the world around you can and will change dramatically. You will see things far more clearly and understand aspects of situations that previously would have passed you by. You will find that sitting at peace and in stillness will become second nature to you, as will dancing.

Second, if there is one thing that appears to remain constant, it is that no matter how urban and worldly the Fae become, their propensity is for tricks and laughter, and more often than not, the joke is on you. Sometimes this can seem malicious, but most times it's not. It just isn't moral in a manner we understand. There are, of course, faeries who act with malice, and there are times when I would suggest that you trust your gut; if it smells a funny color, there is probably a good reason. We have, after all, spent millennia living alongside these entities, so our instincts are unparalleled—we've just mostly forgotten how to use them. If a faery feels malevolent, it's probably best to leave well enough alone for your own health and safety.

The information provided in this book is designed to challenge and stretch your understanding of the world around you. This is not intended to be a "safe" or "comfortable" experience. I will provide words of caution and guidance where necessary, but I cannot be held responsible for your own actions. Please use common sense and perform adequate risk assessments in everything you do. It might seem like a wonderful idea to follow the sound of a selkie singing on a lonely dock, but know the area well before you go wandering off.

Is there a safety risk? Heavy machinery operating? I would like you all to live to tell me wondrous tales of your adventures.

THE SEELIE AND UNSEELIE COURTS

Seelie and unseelie realms are often mentioned in fiction, and the concept can be found as early as the Middle Ages, so there is historical precedent for this form of classification. The word *seelie* comes from the word *sellig*, meaning "blessed." In essence, you may liken "seelie and unseelie" to the concept of "fair and unfair." Many have used the words *light/dark* or *good/evil* to describe the difference, but they always fall foul by using these terms, as no faery, regardless of their type, is truly good or evil (a bit like humans, really). It is entirely possible for a seelie Fae to be mean, spiteful, and downright malicious if it wants to be, just as an unseelie Fae may choose to show compassion.

As a general rule, a seelie Fae is ethically fair, after a fashion, as it is most likely to help rather than hinder. They will inform you of the consequences of any deal you choose to make or break. They will tell you of any offense caused, thus giving you a fighting chance against the incoming problems or, better still, to fix the insult. Meanwhile, the unseelie is wholly self-motivated. They will rarely do anything for a human unless there is something in it for them. They will normally try to trick anybody interacting with them so as to win whatever bargain or bet has been placed, and it takes little if anything at all to offend them; they are wholly unfair in their interactions. The urban Fae fall into both categories.

THE IMPORTANCE OF NAMES

It is not just what court the Fae belong to that you need to consider. When working or dealing with the fair folk, names and lineages can have an important role in how your interactions play out. Consider the following tale.

Once upon a time, there was a very poor miller who had a beautiful daughter. One day, he boasted that his daughter could spin straw into gold. The king heard of this wonder, and he called for the miller's daughter to be brought to the palace. Upon her arrival, he locked her in a room full of straw and gave her a spinning wheel, demanding that she demonstrate her talent. The miller's daughter thought quickly on her feet, saying that she could only work if unobserved. The king left, stating that he would return the following day. If she hadn't completed her task, he would execute both her and her father.

The poor girl was beside herself, and try as she might, she could not spin the straw, let alone turn it to gold. As the first rays of dawn lit the chamber, a little man appeared. He promised to turn all the straw to gold in return for something the girl held precious. The girl, desperate to live, offered the man a necklace her father had made for her. And as quick as a flash, the little man sat down in front of the wheel and spun all the straw into gold.

The king arrived and was astounded by what he saw, but instead of letting the girl go, he took her to an even larger room filled with even more straw. His ultimatum, as before, was certain death if she failed to complete the task. She tried to spin the straw, but to no avail. The little man presented himself again. This time, the girl offered the ring of her dead mother to trade. The little man accepted it and set about the task with phenomenal speed. As morning crept in, the king arrived and viewed the scene with amazement. Yet still he did not grant the girl her freedom, instead escorting her to an even larger room. This time, however, he declared that if the girl completed the task by the following morning, he would make her his queen.

Devastated, the girl realized that she had nothing left to trade. Sobbing with her head in her hands, she waited for dawn. When the little man arrived, she told him that she had nothing left to trade, but the little man instead suggested that he could perform the task in return for a future trade. Hope filled the girl, all caution fled, and she readily agreed to honor any terms he named. The little man smiled mischievously and demanded that, in return for completing the task, she would promise him her firstborn child. Realizing she was trapped, the poor girl could do nothing but agree. The king arrived for the final time and released the girl. A lavish wedding was planned. Despite the weird and dysfunctional start to the relationship, they lived for many years in happiness, the girl forgetting about the promise she had made to the strange little man who had saved her life.

But then came the fateful day. The queen gave birth to a beautiful baby boy, and the entire kingdom celebrated this long-awaited heir. All except for the queen, whose heart was filled with dread of the little man. At sundown, he appeared beside her bed and demanded the child. The queen begged the little man to change his mind. When that didn't work, she offered him all the wealth in the kingdom, but he would not budge. Instead, he gave the queen three days to guess his name. If she failed to do so, he would claim the child on the third night, with or without the queen's blessing.

The queen spent hour after hour trying to guess the little man's name, but to no avail. At dawn, he disappeared. The following day, she spent many hours in the king's vast library, searching for tales of the little man in the hopes of discovering his name, but with no success. On the second night, the same story played out. On the morning of the third day, realizing that all hope was lost, the queen wandered into the dark forest, hoping to find the little man and intending to offer herself in place of the child. She wandered for hours before she came across a small cottage in the woods. Before it, the little man was dancing around in glee, singing to himself, "For shame, for shame, she'll never guess my name, for I am Rumpelstiltskin!"

The queen fled back to the palace and awaited the return of the little man. As if by clockwork, he appeared at dusk, demanding the child. The queen smiled, saying, "Why, Rumpelstiltskin, I think not!" The little man went purple with rage and stamped his foot so hard he fell through the floor, never to be seen again.

Think for a minute about how you would classify Rumpelstiltskin. Unlike many, I would classify him as a member of the seelie court, despite his extortionate, baby-stealing ways. He deals fairly with the girl—a trade for a trade. His behavior is never underhanded or double-crossing, and he gives her a chance to fulfill the deal in a different way when she pleads for leniency—something that may not have happened with a member of the unseelie court. It's certainly food for thought. The difference between the two isn't as simple as it may first seem. This gray aspect is worth being aware of. If the Fae offer you a deal (and they will) and there doesn't appear to be any possible consequence or warning, be careful. Be very, very careful.

"Seelie" or "unseelie" isn't the only way to categorize the Fae and their stories. While the categorization possibilities are many and diverse, eventually a standardized method was devised. It is known as the Aarne-Thompson-Uther Index, and it is used throughout the world. For example, our story above is known as the Type 500 fairy tale. According to the index, Rumpelstiltskin is a "supernatural helper," and his faery name is key to the story.

In the British Isles alone, there are easily a dozen similar tales, which indicates how important names are to the Fae. It doesn't stop in the British Isles, either; the power of knowing a being's true name is a theme that appears across the world. The Jewish faith believes the true name of God is so powerful that its use became taboo to stop any potential abuse of power. Jacob struggled in Genesis with an angel who would not reveal his name, and in some myths, the Egyptian god Ptah created all things by speaking their names. Classical Greek religion and ancient Chinese philosophy all believed in the importance of names, as did many African cultures. In parts of Africa to this day, it is still believed that a person's name can affect how they learn, grow, and behave and even where they stand in society.

Many Fae will work with you without you knowing their true names, often preferring to provide the common nicknames that have been given to them over the years in various locations. Honestly, I would be very surprised if you came across any of the good folk who would willingly give you their real name without first building a long relationship with you. Let's take Jenny Green-teeth, who is a common figure in the folktales found across the North of England. She is what could be called a loathly lady. She's a water spirit with an appetite for young men and boys. For many who come across her and even work with her, she is Jenny, Madam Green-teeth, Jen, or any variation of that name you can think of. In my opinion, there once was a real Jenny who revealed her name. Time and tides have obscured her location and origins, but her memory has lived on in the human consciousness, and her name was then given to all of her kind.

How those names are presented to you is not necessarily straightforward. The world-famous visionary artist and friend to the Fae Brian Froud told a charming tale of a particularly difficult exchange of names in his book *Good Faeries/Bad Faeries*. In it, the faery insisted that it was a dead plant. Repeated questioning and interaction did nothing to clarify the situation. The frustrated and exasperated creature eventually led the artist to a dead plant in his garden; the plant was an honesty. Then all became clear: the faery, of course, was called Honesty![3] The moral of this story is that the Fae can be quite literal, and yet, regularly, not everything is exactly as it seems.

---

3. B. Froud, *Good Faeries/Bad Faeries* (London: Pavilion Books, 1998), 6.

FURTHER CATEGORIZATION OF URBAN SPIRITS

The Aarne-Thompson-Uther Index is amazingly useful for referencing and filing experiences in an academic manner. It will allow you to find information on how to locate certain Fae and what they may agree to do or what their purpose is. Without a doubt, most common folktales are the remnants of some other, older interaction with the faery realms. This background knowledge can be amazingly useful when trying to make connections, as you can often find hints and clues about behaviors and characters embedded in the stories.

Possible tale types you may like to explore to improve your knowledge of the Fae include the following:

- Supernatural Opponents 300–399
- Supernatural or Enchanted Relatives 400–459
- Supernatural Tasks 460–499
- Supernatural Helpers 500–559
- Magic Items 560–649
- Supernatural Power or Knowledge 650–699
- Other Stories of the Supernatural 700–749

However, things get a little difficult with urban Fae, as their lives, stories, and histories have become blurred, and relying purely on academic classifications can be quite limiting. When starting to interact with any entity you come across, you may like to consider using the following higher level of categorization to learn how to progress with an interaction or relationship. The following is a simple three-class system I created that explains the urban faery and how far it has adapted to a more modern environment. It isn't a hard-and-fast rule, but it makes for a neat shorthand when discussing and categorizing urban faery interactions.

- Class 1 spirits: A spirit who seems to have come into existence as a result of an energetic input or group belief. They are often thought-forms who have achieved sentience or dormant Fae who have been reawakened because of beliefs or energy. However, they are so fundamentally changed as a result of the awakening process that no memory of their previous life remains. Conversation with them can be difficult. Their verbal reasoning will often be a big barrier to communication. They tend to express themselves through images rather than sounds.

- Class 2 spirits: Fae who are aware of their previous existence in a natural environment to some small extent. They have changed significantly as a result of human interference or their own desire to adapt. Consequently, their original form or understanding of who they are is flawed. Through work and careful interaction, you can discover their origin. You can converse with them reasonably coherently, but don't expect any earth-shattering oracle or revelations regarding the world of Faerie.

- Class 3 spirits: Fully sentient, fully adapted Fae. They can be witty, funny, charming, spiteful—everything a nature faery can be, but they are 100 percent at home within an urban world. They live in the scum-covered waterways behind abandoned flour mills and sawmills. They lurk behind that 1970s gas fireplace at your auntie's house. You can pass through their gateways via the graffiti you find in dark alleys, if you so wish. They are the things that go bump in the night, and they are most definitely the ones who steal the backs off your earrings.

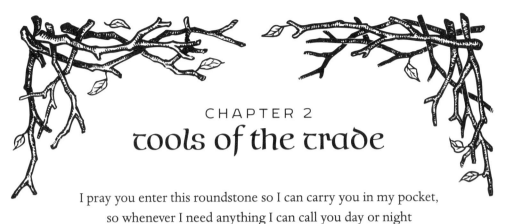

CHAPTER 2
tools of the trade

I pray you enter this roundstone so I can carry you in my pocket,
so whenever I need anything I can call you day or night
and you will always be with me![4]

Much has been said in the Western mystery schools regarding the use of circles, pentagrams, and ritual words to protect the magickal user, but when it comes to the Fae, I truly believe that most of what is currently practiced should be thrown out the window and soundly banished, preferably with laughter.

I have been asked on a number of occasions to help someone get rid of a faery or spirit. Now, obviously, there are times when an entity can cause a lot of trouble, but in my experience, nine times out of ten it is human ignorance that is the biggest problem. We presume that we have dominion over a place because we choose to live, walk, or work there. That couldn't be further from the truth. The Fae have been around at least as long as we have, and probably quite a lot longer. It is we who are the newcomers, the interlopers, the troublemakers. We upset the status quo, and then when we've made a right royal mess, instead of saying sorry, we try to evict our otherworldly neighbors when they complain. Move the problem on and let somebody else deal with it.

Once an understanding has been reached, working with the Fae can be surprisingly simple and, regardless of environment, requires very little paraphernalia. Unlike many other occult practices, it doesn't require a ritual knife, fancy incense, robes, or jewelry. Most of the items you will use, particularly when working in urban situations, are readily available in places like Tesco or

---

4. Paolo Di Sibari, "The Conjuration of the Roundstone," unpublished translation.

Walmart. What you can't buy, you can make, and the most important item of all is free: your mind.

IMAGINATION

It is probably a good idea to start this chapter with a discussion about imagination. It is quite possible that you have wondered if what authors of witchcraft and magick write about is a figment of their imagination. To that I say, of course it is—how could it be anything else? But that doesn't make it any less real, meaningful, or worthy of study.

The skill of imagination is one we have in abundance as children. Yet as adults, our social conditioning relieves us of one of the most valuable magickal skills we will ever possess: the ability to imagine. With our imagination, we can see faeries, goblins, elves, angels, and demons. We can see gods and goddesses and the fantastical realms they all inhabit. With our imagination—the ability to see beyond—we are able to interact with the other. If you can't use your imagination or are not prepared to reclaim it with an open heart and mind, you might as well stop reading now, as imagination will be the most fundamental tool in our adventures with the spirits in the urban world or otherwise.

In nearly every activity you participate in, there are always skills to learn, exercises to perform, and tools to use. When it comes to working with the Fae, ancient lore gives us many examples of gestures, talismans, prayers, ways of wearing our clothing, and even ways of walking that will ensure our safety and hopefully the cooperation of the Fae. However, nowhere I know of is there something that teaches us how to use our imagination, yet using our imagination to interact with the Fae, be they urban or nature-based, will be fundamental to your success.

So, we need to develop this skill first. Let's start by having a go at creating something with our minds, allowing our brains to suspend disbelief and see beyond the physical world in which we live.

FINDING A STORY TO TELL

I had a very active imagination as a child. I often told stories to myself, especially on long journeys. My parents lived in Warwickshire, and my grandparents lived hundreds of miles away in Cumbria. Through my early childhood, I remember endless journeys at the beginning and end of school holidays where we trundled along the motorway between these two destinations. At various intervals along the motorway, there were, and indeed still are, a number of "huts." These constructions are, I believe, designed to house temporary road signs and traffic cones and even to provide some shelter for workers. In the late seventies, these huts were some form of asbestos concrete, painted in green and white. To this day, at least two such structures remain along a section of road that runs between Birmingham and Lancaster.

Cars weren't so fast back then, and journeys were very long. One of the highlights of this journey was seeing the first of these buildings. To my mind, they weren't really workers' huts, but actually secret entries into the world of the Fae. I knew that if my parents pulled over onto the hard shoulder and let me out, and if it was the right time of day, and I knocked in just the right way, when I opened the door, I wouldn't see a dark shed full of shovels and signs and cones. I would see a stairway lit with will-o'-the-wisps, and I would hear the sounds of play and laughter and such wondrous songs. Better still, if I dared to make my way down those stairs, the faeries would be waiting to take me on an amazing adventure.

I am sure you can imagine my surprise when, many years later, I read the wonderful *Artemis Fowl* by Eoin Colfer, a story in which the LEP-RECON units come to the surface of the earth through tunnels from the otherworld. The exits of these tunnels are structures we take to be everyday objects. And then it struck me: of course people who "imagine" would have similar ideas if our imagination is the seed that allows us to see the spirits of place and the realm in which they live. There have to be times when people see the same thing, more or less. After all, how many people see the London Eye or the Golden Gate Bridge every day with their mundane vision? Is it any less likely that those who take the time to imagine and see beyond will see the same things? Of course not; that is why we get common themes in fairy tales and folk stories from all over the world. Our imagination is real!

· EXERCISE ·

memory mood board

Get a poster board and spend a while thinking back to your childhood. Think of a time when you were filled with wonder and a sense of other. You may have a complete scenario like mine. Or you may just remember sensations and feelings—either is okay. Really try to grasp the feelings and list them. Did you shiver? Hear noises? What time of day did those feelings occur? If it helps, draw pictures and stick magazine cuttings, leaves, and pressed flowers onto your board. Daub it in essential oils that evoke those childhood memories—smell is a phenomenally powerful tool in aiding recall. What we are trying to create is what those in the marketing industry call a "mood board."

If the space provided isn't enough, use another sheet. Use as many sheets as you want. Also, if you have a complete story like mine, write it down and try to remember as many details as possible. This should take several sessions. The stronger and more "real" you can make those thoughts and feelings, the better. Interacting with the Fae is not a quick activity; if you rush, you could end up stalled and frustrated or, worse, with certain beings refusing to work with you altogether.

· EXERCISE ·
creating an experience

This exercise requires you to get quite literally pixie-led. Have you ever felt strangely drawn to a particular place while out walking or on a car journey? For example, I have an overwhelming desire to visit the village Kingston Bagpuize. Many times as I have traveled to visit family, it's taken all my willpower not to go flying off in the wrong direction to investigate this oddly named place. I suspect that particular draw may just be because of the name's similarity to a favorite childhood television character (and also because I am just a little bit crazy like that). But it is that kind of overwhelming desire you need to think about.

Find time to act upon a similar kind of desire. Get in the car or on the bus and go to the spooky village you've always wanted to visit. Explore that thing at the end of the industrial estate you work on that seems to call your name when you step outside at lunchtime for some fresh air. Even take a wander down that overgrown alley at the back of the housing complex. Obviously be safe and act within reason; I don't want to hear of people coming to grief as a result of this exercise. But basically, you need to be five years old again and go find yourself an adventure. And as you have your adventure, imagine a story, one in which there is a big sign marked Warning: Dragons Live Here. A sign that you should studiously ignore, by the way.

Ask yourself why you are drawn to venture onward when others would run away. Are you really a changeling? Is it your destiny to help the residents of this strange place fight against the ingress of humanity? Do they have names? What do they look like? Is there a particular time of day or year when their presence in our world is stronger? Do they like certain human foods? Alcohol? Tobacco? Do they have children?

See if you can sense a place or even people in your everyday life who evoke in you the same feelings, smells, memories, or sensations you built during the mood board exercise. Although it's highly likely that some of your own dreams and personality will be integrated into these exercises, it is also equally possible that you are sensing something other, and that your images are coming to you through them. If you do feel that, ask permission to be there, to feel their presence. Let them tell you their story through your imagination.

Make sure to write or draw everything in a notebook. I cannot stress enough the importance of notes. At the very least, I expect your experiences to be included in a short journal entry, something I will go into in more detail later in the chapter. You can repeat these exercises as many times as you like. You may even want to create an experience every time you attempt to make a connection as a way of stripping away the scales of the mundane world that shrouds us all.

ON PAREIDOLIA

Pareidolia is the ability to see faces and shapes in other objects (often things that would be considered nonsentient or inanimate). Not everyone naturally has this skill, but it can be developed, and it tends to become more profound in people who have an active spiritual life. Therefore, some people will find pareidolia easier to achieve than others. Any exercises designed to improve your imaginings are likely to cause an increase in pareidolia, so get used to it. Once you do, it's quite fun.

Psychologists stress that this ability is a remnant of an older monkey mind in which we needed to see things even when there wasn't anything there in order to improve our survival, but that explanation is like throwing the baby out with the bathwater. As we know, when working with the good folk, just because you can't see it, doesn't mean it isn't there.

During your adventures, if you experience pareidolia, go with it. Often it's just a quirky optical illusion, but it can also be an excellent clue as to the location of a faery manifestation.

ON OLFACTORY HALLUCINATIONS

When it comes to recall, one of humanity's strongest senses is the ability to smell. The smell of tobacco may bring back happy memories of your grandfather smoking a pipe, a whiff of a certain aftershave may have you blushing at the memory of your first kiss, and the smell of boiling cabbage can see you breaking out in fearful sweats at the memory of the after-lunch Friday spelling test. These smells may leave you enlivened or crippled with anxiety.

It is not uncommon for strange and often out-of-place smells to assail you when you are in a hotspot of activity. The technical term is *clairalience*, and one of the nice things about this kind of experience is that even the most skeptical person can pick up on these triggers, so if you happen to be walking in a group, ask your companions if they can also smell something, too. If nothing else, it will reassure you that you don't have a life-threatening medical condition!

DOWSING FOR SIGNS
OF ELEMENTAL ACTIVITY

Not everybody is graced with "the sight" 100 percent of the time. Finding that place of other during our adventures in imagination can sometimes feel somewhat anticlimactic if we then can't find a way to easily verify it. For many of us, our sense of the other may be limited to feelings, thoughts, and visions within our inner eye. Time will teach you to trust your gut, and while more often than not we can rely upon our deep intuition—especially if we work with it and hone it—sometimes it can be useful to have a second opinion. This is where dowsing comes in handy, particularly if you use a pendulum.

Dowsing is an ancient skill. While it is most often used to discover lost treasure, water sources, hidden pipes, and, more recently, cables, it can also be used to locate and identify the paranormal, Fae, and other kinds of elemental activity in a particular location.

The main ways to dowse include rods or a pendulum of some form. While there are many suppliers who will sell you a pretty gem on a chain or fancy copper contraptions, you have to remember dowsing is an art that was practiced by our ancestors. It's real hereditary folk magick, and our ancestors weren't people who had access to magnificent online emporiums. They used what they had on hand. A well-balanced pendant, a decorator's plumb line, or a cut-up metal coat hanger can be just as effective. I am rather fond of using a naturally holed stone often called a hagstone for identifying places where the veil thins or Fae frequent, as we have a long and well-documented history of using these stones to see and to protect ourselves from the world of Faerie.

How dowsing actually works is up for debate. Some believe that energetic fields affect the rods or pendulum, causing them to move independently. Others believe that we are the antenna and our focused interactions with the energetic world around us cause minute and involuntary spasms that make the device swing or rotate. I tend toward the latter explanation. I have watched very competent dowsers at work, and sometimes you can see their hands twitch very slightly, causing their tools to move. Regardless, their results are often independently corroborated by other dowsers, so the cry of "I saw your hand move" by the skeptic is a little bit irrelevant if that movement yields verifiable results. Either way, I have found the technique effective enough to use it regularly and for it to be included in this book.

My personal preference is the pendulum. This is partly practical and partly physical. I was first taught to dowse by a lovely elderly gentleman who had been a member of the British Dowsing Society. He made me a set of rods from metal coat hangers. I proceeded to exasperate him for the better part of a morning before we decided that I needed to switch either to a pendulum or to hazel twigs. It didn't matter what we did—changing my grip, insulating the rods by using the bodies of ballpoint pens as handles—the rods either stubbornly refused to move in locations that had been verified by others or would spin wildly out of control the minute I laid my hand on them. I could never get an accurate baseline reading from which to progress. After hours of furrowed brows and gritted teeth, he told me to take my necklace off and try using that as a pendulum instead, and the results were pretty much instantaneous.

I now own a small pair of copper rods with which I do have a reasonable amount of success, so I did finally make further progress, but it goes to show that not every technique suits everybody. I am a firm believer in playing to strengths, not weaknesses, so make sure you try different methods and even materials as you experiment with this technique, because you may have varying degrees of success. For me, the discreet, portable nature of the pendulum is such that it will always be my go-to tool. I always have one in my handbag. After all, you never know when you might need it.

A word of caution: just because we can verify the spirits we have found with these devices, it doesn't mean that we should always take the interaction any further than perhaps an energetic nod of the head or even a small offering—and for some, no interaction at all is best. I will discuss this in more detail in later chapters.

· EXERCISE ·
making and using a pendulum

You can, of course, choose to buy a pendulum to complete this practical activity. But I would recommend you at least have a go at making a pendulum for yourself. Things made with your own hands have an energetic connection to you, often making them far more effective.

You can use something as simple as a hagstone on a piece of string. An old pendant you no longer wear held by its chain is another option. The only real criteria is that there is some weight to the object on the end of the string or chain. This will allow the pendulum to swing well. The chosen weight should also be reasonably balanced, but the weight mustn't be so heavy that the pendulum hasn't ever got a hope in hell of moving anywhere without forceful intervention.

Next, you want to make sure you give the pendulum a good swing about. Get used to how it feels in motion. I don't care what others might say; your crystal isn't going to get dizzy, and it isn't going to turn against you. It is a tool, nothing more. A tool that, if used carefully and with respect, will last you a lifetime, but that is as far as it goes. If you subscribe to the theory that crystals have inherent properties or even indwelling spirits, you need to ask yourself, "Are these properties or beings so fragile that experimental swinging and, indeed, absentminded dangling are going to affect their abilities?" If you answer yes, then you have a fundamental problem. Even ethically mined crystals have been physically wrenched from the earth. A far more traumatic experience than a few twirls, in my humble opinion.

Anyway, moving on. You may wish to charge, bless, sleep with, or consecrate the pendulum. This can be done with running water, moonlight, sunlight, incense, prayers, invoking sigils—any or all are equally valid. But, most importantly, realize that these activities are to help create a bond between you and your tool, so the best thing you can do is use it. You may even find that you do have an indwelling spirit during this period of familiarization, and any of the techniques described in the following chapter can be used to build a working relationship with it. You could even ask a spirit to move into your pendulum, but that's not necessary for it to work.

· EXERCISE ·
calibrating your pendulum

Once you are happy with your pendulum, you need to think of a set of baseline questions that allow you to calibrate your pendulum quickly and easily. This calibration needs to be done each time you use it. The questions can be reasonably simple, such as,

- Am I right-handed?
- Is my name Flossy?
- Is my favorite color pink?
- Is my dog's name Dobby?

The questions you ask must be answered with a yes or no so that you can see what each answer looks like. Some people choose to just ask their pendulums to show them a yes or no movement, and if that works for you, fine. I find I get better results by asking more questions. The pendulum will display the answers in one of two ways: it will move either in a linear motion or in a circular one. A "yes" answer may be given by the pendulum swinging away from you and toward you and a "no" by it swinging from left to right. However, on another occasion, it may rotate clockwise or anticlockwise. Hence the need to check every time you use it.

There is a third state a pendulum can express: that of uncertainty or indecision. The pendulum may display a refusal to move at all or movement that is different from the calibrated answers (linear movement when the yes or no is circular, and vice versa). This can often happen when you have asked a vague question or if there is no answer to give. One of the annoyances (but also blessings) of the pendulum is the need for well-worded, specific questions.

For example, asking a spirit if its name is Fred is going to elicit a strong yes or no, normally. But what if that spirit is a category 1 or 2 spirit and doesn't know or remember its name? A good first question might instead be something like, Do you know your name? I know this all sounds a bit tedious, but it can be surprisingly accurate with a little bit of work and dedication. It also means that there is less room for confusion, and Fae who like to trick or obscure answers are often easier to catch out.

LOCATIONS FOR DOWSING

There has been a massive resurgence in interest in the Fae in recent years. Thanks to the internet, some of the most amazing information has come to light regarding modern faery sightings. The folklorists Simon Young and Cerri Houlbrook conducted something known as the Fairy Census, with data collected from across the world and spanning a number of years.[5] Being academics, they did something that the average "believer" tends not to do too often: they treated all accounts fairly and without bias, which makes for fascinating reading and an excellent resource for any aspiring Fae-workers. One of the most fascinating findings is that you are more likely to have an encounter with a faery in your own home, backyard, or local environment than anywhere else. This essentially blows away the argument that you need to go out to some remote location in nature to make connections with the Fae. It also means that limited mobility need not be an issue, so feel free to just work around your own home with your pendulum. You may be very surprised at what you discover.

Possible locations to consider include the following:

- The bedroom
- The kitchen
- Any fireplace or hearth
- Thresholds (both internal and external)
- Trees or stones in garden spaces
- Woodsheds and other outdoor storage areas

5. Simon Young and Cerri Houlbrook, *Magical Folk* (Croydon, UK: Gibson Square, 2018), 11.

Each home will have a genius loci, a guardian spirit. This is not truly Fae, for it exists almost entirely in this realm, but it does have Faelike aspects. You can sense it, interact with it, give it offerings to help keep the home safe, and so on. In ancient Rome, this energy often manifested in the image of a snake. Don't be surprised once you acknowledge each other if you start catching something out of the corner of your eye slithering out of sight. Another good tell is that the genius loci is often tied to one specific room, whereas other visitors may move around at will.

Some genius loci are fully sentient—others, not so much, but regular work with genius loci or any dormant spirit may awaken them enough that a meaningful relationship can be had. But please read on before you do so. Not everything should be woken. Remember the old saying, "Let sleeping dog lie."

STONES

While it is unlikely that you will readily find some neolithic standing stones when walking down Main Street, it is surprising how often you can find them incorporated into other buildings. Old churches are most often the main candidate for this incorporation. It is thought that the superstitions surrounding these stones were so ingrained in the community that it was easier to incorporate them into Christianity, as destroying them would potentially incur the wrath of their associated spirits.

One such stone is the Romano-Celtic altar stone engraved with a snake goddess that is embedded in the north wall of the local parish church in the town of Ilkley in North Yorkshire; the figure has become synonymous with the river Wharfe, which runs beside the town. Until very recently, locals would process on Mayday from the stone to the river and build a great bonfire, and offerings of flowers were given to the goddess. The Slidey Stane in Holyrood Park, Edinburgh, is quite possibly another such stone. It is said that in ancient times, parents would take their children to this stone and encourage them to slide down it to receive blessings and encourage fertility for the next generation. Although the identity of who was blessing them and assuring their reproductive health is now lost, this is an excellent example of how large rocks and stones containing supernatural powers and potentially faery connections can be found in city environments if you look hard enough for them.

While the belief in these types of spirits has waned in recent generations, some cultures continue to adhere to the old ways regarding the indwelling spirits of rocks. In Iceland, we still see planning departments paying heed to the local people who have declared a certain large boulder or outcropping of rocks an "elf church" and therefore sacred or taboo. Certain Native American tribes believe that stones are a gateway to the otherworld and have many areas that are still sacred. Elsewhere in Europe we see remnants of an older belief, even when no physical stone is present. Arthurian legends suggest that Arthur and his men lay sleeping, entombed in a great rock somewhere on the Cheshire Plain in England, or maybe on the Somerset Levels near Glastonbury, or even in the great forest of Brocéliande in Brittany; each area claiming Arthur's final resting place jests and jibes with gentle rivalry, but the common factor is that he lies entombed in stone.

HAGSTONES AND ROUNDSTONES

Humanity seems inherently hardwired to collect stones. Go walking on a sunny afternoon or spend a day upon a pebbled beach and you can pretty much guarantee that you'll come home with a pocketful of rocks. Well, I do, anyway. It seems that crystals and gems are something that almost everybody is drawn to when they start exploring alternative spiritualities, and for some of us, the draw expands or transforms into a desire to collect grubby bits of flint, quartz, marble, and granite.

We have evidence that this isn't a modern phenomenon. Two thousand years ago, the historian Pliny wrote extensively about something called a serpent's egg much prized by the Gauls.[6] From Pliny's description, it was a snakelike stone believed to have magickal properties. The mythology surrounding its creation is a little vague, but it may have been either a desiccated or fossilized adder that, during the heat of summer, had somehow gotten itself tangled into a knot.

HAGSTONES

The concept of a holed stone having magickal properties seems to be a common theme worldwide. Adder, hag, hex, aggri, Odin, serpent, dobbie, and witch are

6. J. Bostock and H. T. Riley, eds., "Pliny the Elder, The Natural History," Perseus, accessed November 10, 2019, http://www.perseus.tufts.edu/hopper/text?doc=Plin.+Nat.+toc.

just some of the names describing this magickal item that I have come across. The powers they possess are mind-boggling, as are the ways in which they can be used. Common themes are the ability to curse and heal, protection against malignant forces, housing or trapping spirits and forcing them into your service, and—the most common theme across a wide range of cultures—the ability to travel to the otherworlds or underworlds and see the Fae.

The American folklorist Charles Godfrey Leland in his work *Aradia* claimed that to find a stone with a hole in it is "a special sign of the favor of Diana."[7] The charm spoken upon finding the stone claims the stone to be a symbol of good fortune and protection, particularly if combined with rue and valerian. In my experience, a hagstone is a powerful amulet given by the fair folk to aid in both mundane and magickal activities. Hagstones seem to have a finite value or energy, though, and like Tolkien's One Ring, they have a habit of disappearing when their charge has run out. Luckily for us, with the use of quarried materials—particularly flint—in driveways and roads, finding hagstones doesn't always require a special trip to the country or beach.

When you do find a hagstone, hold it to your chest and say the following charm—which is adapted from *Aradia*—three times before working with the stone.

> *I thank fate and the spirit that led me here*
> *so that I should have this stroke of luck!*

You may wish to place the stone on a string or thong around your neck when you head out to work with the Fae. Another alternative would be to place the stone on a keyring. The Museum of Witchcraft in Boscastle has a set of church keys tied on a ribbon with a hagstone attached in its collection, and there is anecdotal evidence that keys of all kinds tied together with hagstones have been used to protect the homes of those who carried them.

Charms, beads, and amulets strung with red thread can be found across Europe, so if you can make your cords or ribbons red, it would be very appropriate to do so. Red seems to relate to the spirits who inhabit stones. Regardless of how you secure the stone—keyring, thong, or ribbon—it can also double as

---

7. C. G. Leland, *Aradia: Gospel of the Witches* (Newport, RI: The Witches' Almanac, 2010).

your dowsing pendulum should you come across an area that feels energetically unusual, as discussed in the earlier section on pendulums.

· EXERCISE ·
using the hagstone

One of the most traditional ways to use a hagstone is to hold the hole up to your eye and stare through. It is supposed to give you the ability to see the faery realms, but if you are expecting some kind of instantaneous shift like you see in *The Spiderwick Chronicles*, I am afraid you will be sadly disappointed. I've not come across anybody who has achieved such a phenomenon working with the stone in this way. What's more, the Fae are renowned for being shy, often appearing to people at the edge of their vision, so this action of directly staring through a hole goes against nearly everything we know about seeing faeries.

Holding the stone up to one eye is also a surefire way to get eyestrain and an arm ache. Although there is sometimes value in maintaining certain poses when performing spells, charms, and other acts of magick, when working with the Fae, it's probably best to be comfortable and fully functional. Therefore, holding the stone in both hands and away from your face is a much more enjoyable solution. Also, it's less likely that you'll get stared at. In this position, the hagstone is a really useful tool to aid in trance workings.

Start by allowing your eyes to defocus on the periphery, and just concentrate on the hole in the stone while performing rhythmic breathing (discussed in detail in chapter 3). You may also want to chant or hum. Following is a charm of calling that is an adaptation of a folk charm from West Sussex, England, which can be repeated almost mantralike until the desired mental state is achieved.

> *Come in the stillness, come to my sight,*
> *hearkening, beckoning, left and right,*
> *come in the stillness, come to my sight!*

Don't spend hours doing this, as you will feel quite physically and mentally drained using this technique. Build up slowly and consider carefully when the ideal time is to use this charm out in the field—in the "get to know you" stage of contact, perhaps? But do practice the technique daily. It can be very rewarding as an energetic and psychic development exercise.

THE ROUNDSTONE, THE BROWNIE STONE, AND THE RED GOBLIN

Another charm found in Leland's *Aradia* is the conjuration of the roundstone. A red goblin (probably the Italian version of a redcap known as a Mazapégul) is bound to the stone with a spoken charm and follows the instructions of the owner of the stone, who carries the stone at all times. A rather interesting take on the genii in a bottle. In the Leland charm, the spirit is instructed to do some rather unspeakable things to people who have offended the caster of the spell. This includes screeching at someone who owes them money until the money is returned and dragging a quarrelsome lover by the hair. Now, obviously, I am not suggesting for one minute that anyone use a spirit for such spiteful ends, but a spirit familiar can be very useful. Years ago, I actually took a picture of the stone gargoyle in which I housed a particular goblin and used it as my avatar on the internet; this effectively gave me the ability to send my goblin almost instantaneously to any location around the world. Very useful as an information-gathering agent.

Leland issues one word of caution, though—one that I echo: "[The red goblin or roundstone] should never be given away, because the receiver will then get the good luck, and some disaster will befall the giver."[8]

The use of stone familiars is not limited to Italian folk magick. Brownies and other household spirits are still very much in existence in our modern urban world, and it has always been considered a good omen to have a brownie or other helper spirit in the house. The Scots kept stones beside their hearths upon which a libation of milk was poured so that the gruagach or brownie (the tales vary) would protect the home against misfortune. In towns and cities, few homes now have a real hearth; should you wish to observe this practice, use the place you consider the heart of your home. You may wish to place the stone to the right of your chosen hearth space, though, for the Cornish pwca apparently sit either to the left or right according to their demeanor, with right being the good side. And a good pwca in your house is always going to be preferable to a spiteful one.

8. C. G. Leland, *Aradia: Gospel of the Witches* (Newport, RI: The Witches' Almanac, 2010), 29.

INVOCATION OF THE STONE

What we can learn from Leland's conjuration of the roundstone is that we essentially need to create a small ritual in which we tie a particular faery to a solid object. Although I would not advocate physical binding, making a tangible magickal connection between an object in your home and any house spirit can be really beneficial. It can mean that any faery who has agreed to work with you has a place to return to should you ask it to leave the household to run errands; the faery can also travel with you should you take a trip or move, thus making it more of a familial spirit than a domestic one.

While in my own practice I have chosen to just provide a stone for my household spirit to live in, many other cultures like to build spirit houses, and old English folklore also discusses the use of a faery throne constructed from hazel twigs. There is quite a provenance behind the idea of spirits being given a place in household objects or statues. Glass mirrors and crystal balls are also mentioned in a number of manuscripts, so, if you wish, you can experiment. See what fits; your house faery will almost definitely have an idea of what it wants, so asking its opinion might be a good idea as well. However, if you choose to house your spirit, there are certain protocols to follow and obligations to meet before you start working together.

First, you will need to decide what is going to be acceptable and maintainable for you. It's no good starting out with cream and fudge every day as an offering if you aren't prepared to keep that up. It's really easy to be gung ho and excited at the idea of your own house brownie who will find your keys and guard the house, but if you can't maintain what you agree on, then the arrangement will end in tears.

Second, the Leland invocation is less like the prayer-style invocations we are used to today and more like a contract: it is an expectation of what the person wants from the Fae entering the stone. The full invocation lists all the things that the finder of the roundstone intends the little red goblin to do for them with no mention of a reward at all. It is dictatorial and commandeering. This manner isn't the most desirable way to work with any house faery. Many don't do so well with being bossed around. This kind of attitude is the most likely reason why so many Fae try to trick us, so mutual exchange is always preferable. That being said, a clear expectation of roles is a must.

Last, consider creating a termination clause in your petition, be that via a certain invocation you create at the start of the relationship or by limiting the length of service to one year, five years, the term of your natural life, and so on. It is highly unfair to ask a being to willingly bind itself with no option to move on should you decide this kind of work is no longer for you, nor is it fair to your family to ask them to look after a spirit after your demise, so think carefully on this before you go on.

You will know when the stone has been inhabited; it will become tangibly heavier in your hand. Once you are happy you've got it right, place the stone where you intend for it to live.

Here is a bare-bones example of a contractual petition you could use and adapt:

Good spirit, I call you,

come to my aid, help me, and do not abandon me in my time of need.

Enter this stone so that you may live with me wherever I go. Protect my home and those who dwell within it, ensuring they come to no harm.

Warn me of people who are not my true friends and all those who wish me ill.

Good spirit, I call you,

come to my aid, help me, and do not abandon me in my time of joy,

and I will feed you once a month with bread and milk and honey.

Enter this stone for a year and a day so that we may grow in trust. Should we find this relationship sound, good spirit, then we may once again agree to a bond of friendship!

I always start my relationships with a short time period and the option to renegotiate. You could go as little as just a few weeks if you wish, but it can take a while to get a house faery to trust, so you'd have to do an awful lot of work for a very short-term agreement. I never specify an exact date for the offering either; once a month allows for flexibility in the time of the offering, which means you aren't going to suddenly have an irate brownie because you have to go away for a few days and upset their routine by making the offering early or late.

Should the relationship prove successful, then after the initial contract has expired, you may choose to petition the Fae again with additional requests. As before, state what you want from them, the payment terms, the length of the contract, and any other clauses as you see fit. Remember to start giving the offerings in the manner in which you agreed before you need to call upon them. Think of it as a down payment. It is a sign of good faith and trust.

THE ETHICS OF COLLECTING STONES

I would like to end this section with a thought about the ethics around collecting stones. In the United Kingdom, it is actually illegal to collect stones from certain beaches, although sea glass is considered fine. In other areas, authorities will turn a blind eye to the odd stone being collected here and there, but lately this tolerance seems to be becoming less and less. People are now aware of the unethical mining of crystals and are increasingly looking to harvest beaches for less glamorous stones that they can use raw or even tumble to create beautiful items for jewelry and healing.

The problem is that if everybody does this, we could be creating yet another problem. All along the south of England, coastal erosion is becoming a risk to people's homes and livelihoods, and certain local councils have had to make hard decisions as to how they can preserve the coastlines and the precious maritime ecosystems they contain. It's not just a case of letting one beach get washed away by the tides; it's also where that beach will be deposited and whether it will affect surrounding wetland and wildlife as a result.

So, although it is really tempting to head straight to the beach to find yourself a bag of hagstones, roundstones, or a nice large brownie stone, please think carefully. The reasons so many cultures prized these items were because they were unusual or rare. Waiting can make an object far more meaningful. Also, because we are inherently magpies and collectors, should you find a hagstone you like "better," consider returning your old stones when you are finished with them, even if you didn't find them at the beach.

THE FAERY FIELD JOURNAL

I hated writing a magickal diary when I started on my path, and it was pretty much a requirement of my training, so the fact that I *had* to do it made it even more awful. But I cannot stress how grateful to myself I am that I kept it up and that I am now able to look up past encounters and experiences (and how often I kick myself at half-remembered rituals or adventures that I didn't bother documenting, of which I am now unable to recall fine details—details that are always all of a sudden vitally important when I try to remember them).

I really wish bullet journaling had been a thing back then. I think I would have embraced the whole idea of the faery field journal far quicker. I have an entire shelf of journals, files, and binders, but it is really only the last few years' worth that I find of use, because there was a level of love and creativity that went into the making of them (along with the strategic use of indexing; never underestimate a good index). Hopefully your experience will be far more pleasant and fun than mine initially was. What I need is for you to make a habit of recording your experiences. It will allow you to find patterns and meaning in your work and readily access information that may be key to building a connection with a particular Fae. It may even give you the clues on how to sever a connection, if you have to.

RATIONALE

The reasons behind keeping any magickal diary or journal are many. On its own, it can become a talismanic object charged with your power and the power of the things you write and place within its pages. Don't underestimate this. When I set out for an adventure, I have key items in my day sack: journal, pen, pencil, whittling knife, wand, and so on. The ritual of placing them into the bag, touching them, and remembering the last time they were used can place you into a state of readiness, making you more receptive. My journal is part of that. It often gets examined and touched, opened, and read briefly just before it goes in. It's a great energetic trigger.

A journal is also a record or study of events that can be used later. Recording on the scene is likely to be far more accurate than anything written after the event. I've tried using electronic devices such as journaling and handwriting apps on a phone or small tablet out in the field, and this hasn't proved to be very successful. Assuming the batteries don't inexplicably drain (which does happen) or the heavens don't open, you normally have to walk away from the scene of the experience to sit and use the devices without risk of damage. Faery glamour works very effectively, and once outside of their sphere, it can be very hard to recall exactly what happened. I distinctly remember one such incident some miles from my home where, in the early hours of the morning, my friend and I came across an unusual "person" at a crossroads. To this day, all we can agree on is that he was probably Greek and was riding a push-bike. We have no accurate recollection of how he was dressed. I claim he was wearing a very sharp three-piece suit, my companion claims not. Nor do we recall where exactly he was going, only that he asked for directions.

While both of us immediately knew we had encountered somebody not of this world, neither of us thought to stop there to write the details down. It was very late; we were tired after ritual, and there was still a two-mile walk home. We didn't discuss it properly—other than to laugh about the strangeness of the encounter—until the next day. But by then, the damage was done, and our memories clouded.

Before you get too caught up, write something. It doesn't have to be an essay. If you are at all artistically minded, then as you become more proficient at interacting with the otherworld, you may find you prefer to mostly draw rather than write. It was a revelation to me to realize quite how much information I could capture this way. A look, an atmosphere, fragmented images that made no sense at that time but would come back later with meaning or repeat themselves until I "got it." At the very least, the following points need to be recorded in some way or another to be of value at a later date.

- Date and time
- Weather
- Lunar cycle
- Location
- Thoughts and feelings
- Conversation/words/internal dialog

Truthfully, I don't care if your journal is typed on a computer, scribbled on a tablet, or written in fine copper plate italics with a Mont Blanc fountain pen; you just have to write things down as soon as possible. Try a whole bunch of different ways of recording this information. A voice recorder or even a GoPro could also be a valid documenting tool if you can make it work for you. Just because I've not had much joy with electronic goods, doesn't mean you won't. We are urban adventurers seeking urban Fae. Modern technology isn't a no-no; just make sure you have a backup notebook and that you archive your files in such a way that you can search easily for specific themes, experiences, or incidents and cross-reference.

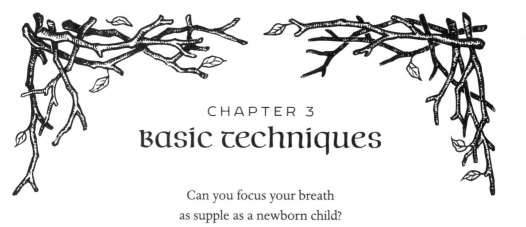

CHAPTER 3
Basic Techniques

Can you focus your breath
as supple as a newborn child?
Can you cleanse your vision
till there is no blemish?[9]

As previously mentioned, working with the Fae requires precious few tools or formal rituals in comparison to other systems of magick or spirituality. However, although our ancestors can inform us through the folklore and mythology that they have left behind, the adaptive nature of urban Fae means that, in some ways, we have to work far more intuitively than many practitioners on more structured paths. This doesn't mean that we can totally ignore the basics, though. When you look across many of the most successful world religions and practices, there are core components that persist regardless of belief, and this is for a very good reason. They work!

In this chapter, we shall look at a few components that will aid you in your explorations.

BREATHING TECHNIQUES

Meditation and breathing are two of the most powerful techniques you can practice when you are intent on exploring the unseen worlds. The right exercises can enhance your existing psychic skills, allowing you to be more sensitive to the entities around you. They can even allow previously hidden powers to surface naturally. Results can be achieved in just a few minutes a day, but as with anything, the more you do it, the better you get.

---

9. Lao Tzu, "Tao Te Ching," translated by Soon Teo, Tao Te Ching Made Easy, accessed October 2019, https://tao-in-you.com/tao-te-ching-quotes/.

If you take time to go to a meditation group, listen to online resources, or read books on the subject of meditation and breath work, it won't be long before you come across a statement such as, "Take some time. Work with your breath for a while." If you've been unlucky and hit this milestone early on in your learning, then you probably sat there for a bit, contemplating this statement. Are you supposed to be following a specific pattern? Is it supposed to be actual work? Is it a thing you've not been taught yet? Are you doing it right? Nine times out of ten, by the time you've processed this all, you've let the monkey mind win, and you're a long way from that lovely alpha state of being you were trying to achieve.

What does "working with your breath" actually mean? As a standalone statement without further instruction, not a lot. It's a bit of a rookie mistake that new and inexperienced instructors make, which is to assume that everybody is at the same level of experience and understanding. It can be really off-putting. In an attempt to not fall into the same trap, I would like to take a moment to clarify so that we are all coming from the same place.

· EXERCISE ·
practice breathing

There are many different types of breathing exercises, and each technique achieves different things. The fourfold breath, for example, is supposed to reduce anxiety and stress and is often taught as part of mindfulness courses. The 4-7-8 pattern aids in rapid, deep relaxation intended as a prelude to sleep. Alternate nostril breathing is often deployed at the end of certain yoga classes and can either leave you mentally alert or completely relaxed depending on the pattern. The list is endless. But let's break down a couple of the more common techniques just to make them a little clearer.

FOURFOLD BREATH

Breathe in for the count of 4
Hold for the count of 4
Breathe out for the count of 4
Hold for the count of 4

4-7-8 BREATH

Breathe in for the count of 4

Hold for the count of 7

Breathe out for the count of 8

I encourage you to give these exercises a go, but please be aware that with both of these techniques, your lung capacity, physical health, and fitness can play a part in whether you can achieve these patterns. For example, I tend to not perform a fourfold breath because, thanks to years of smoking in my teens and twenties, I now have a less-than-optimal lung capacity. If you are struggling, try a threefold breath instead. You can always work up to these patterns— something that is also often left out of the proverbial instruction leaflet when you go to classes.

Without a shadow of a doubt, practicing breathing exercises has value. There has been a lot of research into the use of sound, breathing, and meditation, and some experiments have even demonstrated that these techniques allow us to change our brain wave frequencies. Science is slowly catching up with what yogis, wise folk, witches, and magicians have known for years.

In a fully conscious state, our brain waves naturally operate at about fourteen to thirty cycles per second. This is known as the beta state. When we meditate, we can reduce these frequencies to about seven to fourteen cycles per second. This is the same frequency found in people when they experience the paranormal senses clairaudience, clairvoyance, or clairsentience. This is known as the alpha state. Furthermore, if you can reduce your brain waves into the four to seven frequency—and some people, such as Zen masters and yogis, can—you enter a highly creative state. This is known as the theta state. It is at the lower end of alpha and at the top end of theta that you are most likely to start communicating with or journey to the otherworld. It is very possible to achieve those states using various technologies, such as binaural and hemi-sync, but they can also be obtained through breathing practice and meditation.

Therefore, when we are working with the Fae and attempting to contact them on their frequency, using these skills seems pretty obvious—but which one? There is actually a whole host of Eastern practices, breathing patterns, and mudras that can help. I encourage everyone to explore these techniques. They are very effective, and you may well find something that you really connect to.

Mostly, these are beyond the remit of this book, so I've included some recommended reading if you want to explore more. However, here are some very simple drills that I was taught by one of my first mentors. They don't require detailed knowledge of other cultures, and they are easy to achieve, even if your lung capacity is limited.

· EXERCISE ·
rhythmic breathing

This technique should be the foundation of every meditation, journey, ritual, and act of magick you ever undertake. As with many breathing exercises, there is a pattern to follow, but you can set that pattern to suit you.

In simple terms, a rhythmic technique will consist of an inhale of a set length followed by a hold of exactly half the inhale. The exhale will be the same length as the inhale, followed by a hold that is, again, exactly half. I recommend starting with a 4-2-4-2 pattern and building up from there if you feel you need to or just like to overachieve.

The point of this exercise is that we start everything we do on a level playing field. Our inner system is calm, we are not in any heightened state of emotion that may affect our results, and we can observe all that is going on around us objectively. When you first start, you may take several minutes or even more to achieve this detached calmness, and this is where many people can fall down, believing the technique to be impractical when working outdoors in inclement weather and especially on busy streets and in other urban locations. However, as time goes on, like a well-trained dog, your body and mind will recognize the patterns and switch into gear very quickly, perhaps with just six or seven cycles, making this technique quick, simple, and efficient. You can hang around on a street corner waiting for an Uber longer than that, and nobody notices. It really is a case of sticking to it.

MANTRA AND TRANCE

Other ways of leveling the playing field and adjusting our brain waves can also be very effective. Both movement and sound can achieve the desired results if you find that a sitting practice is not for you. One of my most favorite ways to shift headspace at home is to work at my spinning wheel. It combines both repetitive sound and movements. Obviously, most people do not have a wheel in their homes, so the following are exercises that can be achieved in some form or another by most people.

· E X E R C I S E ·
rhythmic walking

Have you ever walked for a prolonged period of time with no particular place to go? Maybe singing a snippet of a song or repeating some words that pop into your head like a mantra? You can easily achieve a light trance state without even realizing it; your journey suddenly becomes a blur, and you have little recollection of how you reached your destination. What you were doing is the early stages of what I have coined "rhythmic walking."

There are certain times of day that make this more effective if you are in an urban environment—dawn and dusk, for example, particularly on stormy days. The wind adds a white noise to your activity, drowning out many of the discordant sounds associated with busy streets; the cars rattle past you like the rumble of prayer wheels, adding to the atmosphere. The half-light and the regular strobing of car headlights will put you firmly into a trance, one that will allow you to see things on those busy streets that other people miss. We are so busy and closed off that even the strangest of fellow commuters are ignored as if they are not there, and yet there they are, and it takes so very little to see and feel them.

This is the foundation of many of the skills used in Western mystery schools that employ movement and chanting to "raise energy," but few realize that, if done well, they completely change your brain wave patterns, allowing you to enter alpha or even theta patterns and making you more receptive.

Next time you are out, try using the following chant. It doesn't have to be loud; it can be whispered under your breath, but try to make some sound.

> *In stillness and movement, come to my sight,*
> *hearkening, beckoning, left and right,*
> *in stillness and movement, come to my sight!*

When performing this exercise, you don't have to be walking fast. Try walking at various speeds, and if you are unable to walk, try doing this exercise when you are a passenger in a car on a fast motorway. Another interesting place to try this is on a bridge spanning a busy road. Bridges, like crossroads, are liminal places—great locations for potential Fae encounters. The thundering of the traffic below moving up through your chest cavity, combined with well-timed rhythmic breathing, means that you don't even need to walk. One word of caution with this final suggestion, though. We live in sad times, and people below may see someone who is peering down to the traffic below as a soul in need of help and call emergency services, so consider how and where you will place yourself to ensure this doesn't happen.

Once you find that your trance is deep enough and a connection is made, certain key signs will appear to you. A strange buzzing sensation, almost like the onset of pins and needles; rubbish appearing from nowhere, chasing you down the street and whipping around your legs; a change in air pressure, causing ears and sinuses to pop; and even an almost supernatural reduction in noise levels are all indications that you are getting this right and that you are now, quite literally, walking the line between here and the other.

· EXERCISE ·
the silence between

The following exercise is not one easily achieved outdoors; it also takes you a level deeper than just the light trance of rhythmic breathing and walking. As such, you may wish to limit it to times when you are working with your house spirits and domestic Fae or as part of your scrying experiences at home.

On the upside, one of the nice things is that, to start with, you can do this exercise tucked up in bed. Morning or evening, it doesn't matter. The important part is that you are relaxed and comfortable, warm and undisturbed. It can be combined with a short nidra exercise if you already do that form of mindfulness.

As a health warning, if at any time you become concerned about your heart rate, stop and seek out medical advice.

STAGE 1

Start the exercise lying on your side. You may want to experiment with which side you prefer. Physical limitations can sometimes play a part here. Press your ear firmly against your mattress or pillow. Breathe slowly and regularly, but do not worry about any rhythm or pattern. Just focus on the sound of your heart beating in your ear, the blood pumping through your veins. Allow your breathing to sync with this most primal and mystical of tides. The ebb and flow of the essence of life, your blood. For the first week or so, that is all you need to do. Become accustomed to your own natural rhythm and how your heart sounds.

STAGE 2

Next, you will want to build on the awareness of your heartbeat and the blood pumping through your body. To achieve this, you will need to learn to take your pulse. This is simply done by placing two fingers on the thumb side of your wrist, almost directly below the fleshy part of your thumb. Some people have stronger pulses than others, so a little bit of experimentation may be required, but stick with it.

When you are comfortable with consistently measuring your pulse, the next step is to do this while also lying on your side and listening to your heartbeat in your ear. After a few attempts, you will find that the beat in your ear is just fractionally out of rhythm with the pulse in your wrist. For this week, you need to take time to focus on that fraction of a second, the stillness between the beats. Become familiar with the "silence between."

STAGE 3

The purpose of this whole exercise is to teach you to access a space beyond reality. Doing so with your own body as the portal means that you can effectively tether yourself to this reality with your own heartbeat as the anchor, making this a very safe form of journeying. This week, your primary task is to use your imagination to sense what is in that silence between the beats. Sense the gap between the heartbeat and the pulse as a doorway opening and closing for just that split second. Watch this play out in your mind's eye as if you were looking through a scrying mirror, and notice that the longer you watch, the longer the images seem to last. Imagine this like a strobing effect: there is a gap between each image, but the brain starts to fill in the gaps between, making one constant stream of data. At this point, your awareness of your heartbeat and your pulse will fade. That is to be expected, so let it happen. For now, don't try to analyze the images; it isn't necessary. Just let the scene unfold in front of you. Enjoy the ride, and when you are ready, focus again on your heartbeat and pulse to return to the here and now.

STAGE 4

Finally, when you are ready, you may choose to step through the portal and completely immerse yourself in the otherworld, for that is where you are when you enter the silence between. This is a place we both inhabit—neutral ground, Fae and human alike. It's a place where we can interact on a level playing field. It's best visited when you have a purpose, though, for wandering through the edges of Faerie aimlessly is a surefire way to lose your grip on reality.

Always take note of where you have traveled and retrace your steps faithfully. If you have made a deal or a bargain with any being along the way, please honor it before you return through the silence, or if it is agreed that you will do so within a particular time frame, please don't forget, or you may find your next journey not quite so pleasant.

· EXERCISE ·
the verdant breath

Ivy is a very hardy plant; it grows pretty much anywhere, even in some of the most heavily polluted areas. It is renowned for its filtering properties and is a great oxygenator. Just type "ivy and Chernobyl" into your favorite search engine, and one of the first images is a wonderful picture of verdant green leaves engulfing a tree in the exclusion zone. Ivy can climb and make a wonderful screen, living in relative harmony with the trees and buildings that it grows upon. It has one of the highest ratios of indwelling spirits I have ever encountered, so it's quite possibly the first plant Fae you will make contact with in the urban world.

This makes ivy the perfect symbol of cleansing and protection. The following exercise forms an integral part of my daily protective ritual, but it can be performed on its own very effectively when you just wish to tune in to the world around you.

1. If you can, buy a small ivy plant. This might help with this exercise as you can hold it and build a connection with the essence of the plant. You can also visualize it or just pick a small amount while out for a walk; it lasts quite well. We are symbiotic beings with the plants and trees that share this planet. We more or less breathe in oxygen and breathe out carbon dioxide. Plants take in that carbon dioxide and other pollutants and

convert them back to oxygen. We can use the spirit of ivy to cleanse and ground ourselves, not just the gases we breathe.

2. Sit or, preferably, stand with your back straight and allow yourself to breathe rhythmically for a while, just holding the plant in your hand or in your mind's eye.

3. When you are ready, take a deep breath by whatever way is normal for you and expel all the air completely. You may want to do this a couple of times.

4. Slowly and consciously begin to inhale. As you do, imagine drawing a rich, green, clean, purified energy from the plant in through your nose.

5. Hold the inhalation for a moment. Imagine the energies mixing in your body and spreading to every part of yourself and your aura, pushing any dark, negative energies back toward your nose as they go.

6. Exhale with an *aum* sound, imagining your breath carrying any blockages or negativity from your body toward the plant spirit, who will cleanse it before releasing it back into the universe.

7. Repeat steps 4–6 for at least 7 breaths or for as long as you like.

Once you have performed this exercise a few times, don't be surprised if you become attuned to the signature of ivy. You will probably notice your plant has its own particular energy pattern and that it fluctuates and changes as you exhale, feeding it your waste energy. Once this happens, don't be surprised if you notice ivy everywhere in places you frequent on a daily basis. Climbing on walls, growing in gardens, curling around tree trunks in your favorite park; the colors, shapes, and varieties will also astound you, leaving you wondering why you never noticed the ivy before. You will find that you no longer need an actual plant to perform this exercise. You will be able to sit for just a moment and visualize the ivy, feeling its essence as if it were right in front of you. Also, as you exhale, you are exhaling to a greater whole, to all ivy everywhere. The sense of symbiosis and connection can be quite astonishing. It is then that your first Fae contact may happen spontaneously.

It is my belief that all plants, trees, rocks, rivers, and so on have the ability to contain an indwelling spirit. It is more than a soul; it is a unique and conscious entity in its own right that is potentially linked with the plant soul. Something akin to the concept of the dryad found in certain trees. These beings are, in my opinion, of the world of Faerie. But they are closer to our world than certain other species, for they have a physical connection to this realm in the form of the organic object they inhabit, so it takes little for us to make a tangible connection. Even so, to see these beings, we have to be able to shift our consciousness just a little bit further down into the alpha band of wavelengths. To achieve this, several mystery schools use a color countdown similar to the one on page 47, the most famous probably being the crystal countdown used by the phenomenal witch Laurie Cabot. This countdown has been the basis of the training of quite literally thousands of witches. It is almost without a doubt based on the work by Robert Monroe, founder of the Monroe Institute and researcher into altered states of consciousness.

After having used this technique for some time, I experienced a flare-up of osteoarthritis, which I have suffered from since my early twenties, and I could no longer comfortably cross my fingers to achieve the "instant alpha" encoding. Additionally at that time, the medication I was prescribed temporarily affected my ability to visualize effectively, so I started searching for an alternative way of shifting my brain down into alpha that didn't require me using headphones and prerecorded music. The clue was in the hand mudra used to activate the third eye and pineal gland. Cabot's technique requires that you cross the middle finger over the index finger, whereas the yogic buddhi mudra, also known as the seal of mental clarity, just requires you to touch your thumb to your little finger—far more achievable with stiff hands. Further experimentation also revealed that even when my visualization was at its worst, I could still happily sense my internal chakras, making the whole exercise far more user-friendly, both for myself at the time and for people beginning their training. Once in alpha, the brain compensates for the lack of visualization in the beta state, which is also a boon.

· MEDITATION ·
the third eye opening

- Call to the spirit of ivy to aid you, close your eyes, and follow the verdant breath exercise.
- Place your hands into the buddhi mudra (seal of mental clarity).
- Keeping your eyes closed, slowly count through the chakras.

~ If you can, see the color red and sense your root chakra.

~ If you can, see the color orange and sense your sacral chakra.

~ If you can, see the color yellow and sense your solar plexus chakra.

~ If you can, see the color green and sense your heart chakra.

~ If you can, see the color blue and sense your throat chakra.

~ If you can, see the color violet and sense your third eye chakra.

~ If you can, see the color white and sense your crown chakra.

• Now, imagine a brilliant violet star or a warm sensation shining a beam of light into your pineal gland, activating your third eye and encouraging clear sight and psychism.

• At some point, you will feel an odd floating or dropping sensation, and it is at this point that you are ready to start sending your awareness out to sense any denizens of the other realms: dryads, brownies, devas, and so on. They may be in your local area.

• When you are ready, break the mudra and allow your mind to focus back onto your heartbeat and breathing. At this point, you may wish to take seven large, deep breaths, exhaling audibly each time.

Once you are happy that you can quickly and efficiently achieve an alpha or light trance state of being, you should experiment with other triggers to see if something else suits you better. Some people find that a word or combination of breaths has the same result. Remember, this is your path, and once you understand the mechanics of a thing, there is no reason why you can't refine or change it to suit you.

CHAPTER 4

Being careful

One night she turned her clothes inside out,
turning clothes being as effective as Iron or holy water
when repulsing Fairies.[10]

Generally, society as a whole has forgotten what it takes to coexist with the other realms, and this is the single biggest reason why we no longer see the good folk or interact with them as we once used to. Humanity has developed an arrogant attitude that we are at the top of the food chain, in control of what we do, what we see, and what we interact with. Because of our egocentric culture focused on "me" and "I want," we are disconnecting ourselves from the world around us, and Western cultures in particular have become masterful at creating that disconnect. Despite living in an age in which spirituality is gaining increasing importance, we seem to pay lip service to the idea of the otherworlds, but only if they are serving or directly beneficial toward us. Visit any blog, forum, or social media group and search for the words *sage* and *smudging* or *banish*, *cleanse*, *purify*, and *purge* to see what I mean. No matter how enlightened we may feel, we have barely stepped away from the concept of banishing evil, with "evil" being defined as anything you feel uncomfortable with or that doesn't do as it's told. The problem is, much of the otherworld makes us feel uncomfortable, at least until we come to know it. It is, in essence, what defines it as "other": an alien nature or energy different from our own. Something that we cannot easily categorize and define.

Being careful isn't about entering a new space or place and smudging the living daylights out of it, nor is it about magick circles, boundaries, salt, or

10. B. Froud and A. Lee, *Faeries* (New York: Harry N. Abrams, 1978).

molasses—although, from time to time, we do need to know how to use those things effectively. Being careful when we make contact almost never requires us to bark orders, challenge with swords, or demand obedience.

SENSIBLE PRECAUTIONS
AND WHEN TO USE THEM

That all being said, before we go further, it is important we talk about appropriate cleansing, warding, protection, and defenses. I don't think you will read a book on the occult that doesn't give you a daily protection or meditation ritual, and that is for good reason. But how many of us actually do more than give safety lip service on a daily basis? In my experience, warding and protection get the same treatment as breathing and meditation; many people really only make the barest attempts to keep themselves and their environs spiritually "clean" and "secure." This normally happens when they feel a problem has arisen. Then, their approach is a bit like the frantic blitz spring-cleaning that so often happens when the in-laws or the boss is coming over for the evening. It is reactive rather than proactive. And I am probably just as bad as everybody else.

At the very barest of minimums, you may want to consider a simple daily cleansing ritual and a weekly renewing of the boundaries about your home. The Fae tend to be attracted to those who work with them, and it isn't uncommon for them to multiply and become something of a nuisance if you don't put adequate security in place.

CREATING AND MAINTAINING A BOUNDARY

Have you ever had a totally rubbish day at work and come home so drained you want to cry? I have many times, and I've also felt a million times better after a hot bath and something to eat. "Well that's just fatigue," I hear you say. Not always. Sometimes people can drain you; they get into your personal space, they get under your skin, they make life difficult, and once that energetic line has been crossed, it can be hard to put boundaries into place to stop them from doing it again.

Think about the days when it has been you who is the psychic vampire: you left home late, maybe your partner or kids riled you up first thing in the morning, the dog pooped in the kitchen and you stepped in it on the way to make coffee, and, worse still, your car wouldn't start. Whatever it was, it put you in an energetically foul and aggressive mood. The minute you walked into the office, the atmosphere changed. Colleagues you normally laugh and joke with became sullen and snappy, and your normally happy-go-lucky boss wasn't interested in your excuses and gave you the worst job of the day because you missed morning meeting. The situation spiraled out of control, and by the end of the day, everyone was making audible sighs of relief as they practically ran for the door, not making eye contact or saying farewell, and you knew it was you who had made that atmosphere. Admit it, you've been there. I know I have.

How do we stop this from happening? Well, as the age-old saying goes, the best offense is a good defense, and when it comes to working with energy and nonhuman entities, never a truer phrase was spoken. Banishing everything in sight and calling it cleansing and protection is not the answer. Think! If our lack of energetic boundaries can affect us and those around us in our mundane life, imagine how it may affect those spirits from the otherworlds. Our best cleansing, warding, and protection should be for ourselves. Not only do they stop others' negativity from affecting us, but we are also being mindful that this world is more than just us; we are being polite and respectful neighbors.

It's not all about keeping the bad things out, either. The point of daily cleansing and protection is multilayered.

Here are some benefits of daily protection rituals:

- Personal psychic protection
- Personal energetic protection
- Calming and balancing
- Clarity of thought
- Protection of the environment around you
- Protection of the entities around you

PERSONAL PSYCHIC PROTECTION

This is the area most often covered in books and face-to-face training: the need to protect one's mind from normally unnamed or unseen forces that linger on a daily basis if you work with any form of spirit or occult energies. If you are invoking every day, calling out to the unseen and unknown, then there are going to be times when those things don't leave as planned. The very act of working with the Fae does attract additional strange and unusual entities. Whether they are being attracted to you or you just see them more is up for debate, but the outcome is the same: more phenomena to deal with.

Never fear, though. The reality is that, if you are just going about your daily life, your average bogieman isn't going to pay attention to you unless you start poking at it. As most folks do not have the time or energy to go talking with every single Fae they meet on a daily basis, the primary reason for doing these rituals is to fortify your psyche to deal with any entities you are wanting to work with when you do have the time and inclination. A strong mind is fundamental to this work, and a daily ritual designed to protect yourself and flex your psychic muscles is unquestionably the most important tool you will ever have when working with the Fae.

PERSONAL ENERGETIC PROTECTION

Psychic and energetic protection can be so closely connected that it is sometimes hard to differentiate between the two. It is possible to work with a spirit (or even a person) who may either intentionally or unintentionally drain your energy; they are often called psychic or energy vampires. Brain fog and confusion are often reported when people encounter these beings. As a rule, this isn't so much because of the spirit or person trying to tamper with your circuitry, but just the result of the tiredness and general malaise that happen when you find yourself with a low energy reserve from being in their presence. We've all experienced the sensation, that overwhelming tiredness at the end of a long, hard day. Our brains just switch off, and we find it hard to focus on what we should be doing. Reading, watching TV—all the usual things are suddenly too hard to bother with.

This phenomenon is, in my opinion, the basis of many tales of time and memory loss reported in faery sightings old and new. So, just as it is important to strengthen the mind shields, it's even more vital to work on the body shields, too. And while the ritual on page 55 is one and the same for both psychic and energetic well-being, the component parts have different purposes. Performing daily protection rituals and visualizations helps build the mind, and the breathing and energy work strengthen the energetic field and body shields.

There are plenty of people who sit day after day just running through the motions. If you've ever been to any form of psychic development class, you've probably come across them. Week after week, the spirits will tell a particular person that they need to work on their shielding, and week after week they proclaim loudly that they are. What they are doing is just mentally listing their chosen protection ritual in their heads without ever really "feeling" it. Consequently, while they are very strong-willed, strong-minded people, if you were to poke them energetically, it would take seconds to breach their energetic shields, sap them of their energy, and leave them confused and easy to manipulate. Not that I am advocating this, of course, but now that you are aware of it, just take time to observe some of the most strong-willed people you know, especially those who you know practice some kind of daily meditation or protection. How many of them still feel unbalanced and off-kilter? I think you might be surprised.

Being able to isolate the psychic from the energetic when working with the Fae (or in any other magickal situation) can be really useful. In complicated or stressful situations, banging up your psychic shield can be like throwing up a smoke screen; it leaves you as blind as the spirit or person you are hiding from. And that isn't always desirable. What you really want is to be nicely protected but with all the communication channels open and a good, clear view of what is going on around you. Being able to tweak your shielding to different levels depending on the circumstances is vital.

CALMING AND BALANCING— CLARITY OF THOUGHT

Many folk still feel like they don't "get" meditation, and they get fixated upon the mechanics, missing the point entirely. Yet meditation is no great mystery, and is not just the remit of wise Eastern yogis and Buddhist monks. In Celtic and Norse mythology, we have documented evidence of meditation techniques being performed. In the Norse poem *Hávamál*, Odin hung for nine days and nine nights in order to obtain the knowledge of the runes. In Welsh mythology, the demigod Llew Llaw Gyffes also hung suspended in total stillness in order to achieve enlightenment and transformation. Druids meditated in darkness with a stone upon their chests or wrapped themselves in the hide of a bull to achieve altered and enlightened states. Even in faery lore, we hear of people who intentionally chose to dance around various faery rings or sacred places in order to travel to elfland.

Of course, we don't need to hang from a tree and lose an eye or change into an eagle and drip maggots to achieve positive results. Neither do we need to spend years in an ashram or seek out mind-altering fungi. At the most basic level, meditation is taking time out of your day to just sit and breathe, to allow your mind to stop racing with the million thoughts that bombard it. A very nice side effect to incorporating a daily cleansing and protection routine into your life is that many daily protection exercises are entirely meditative and internal, so if anybody asks what you are doing, you can say it's self-development or self-care, and even the most skeptical relative or friend will give you the green light. If you keep your mind and body clear and protected, you cannot help but feel calmer and more balanced.

Once you sit, and breathe, and calm your mind, it becomes very easy to see solutions and to work wholeheartedly on the things that matter. It is grounding, and it's so much harder to be unintentionally pixie-led if your feet are firmly planted, both physically and energetically, in the here and now.

PROTECTION OF THE ENVIRONMENT AND ENTITIES AROUND YOU

For the most part, it's fair to say that we nearly always assume it's about us—that we are the most important thing in any situation, that our feelings count more than anyone else's. When I find myself slipping into this mindset, I cannot help but cringe inside. I am mortified and want to crawl away in embarrassment. We weren't the first sentient beings on this earth, and I sincerely hope we aren't the last. And just because some of our coinhabitants on this sparkly blue rock don't always share the same reality as us, doesn't mean they aren't important, too. Practicing protection should never be just about us alone. When we try to step into the spaces between—to peer through the veil, to talk to the other—we are making little ripples, and little ripples can turn into big waves. If we go unshielded into the space of the Fae, we can wreak havoc for them as well as for us.

I have often thought (although it's very hard to get a faery to help me test the theory) that the reason faeries hate iron so much is because it's such a great conductor that's more than capable of breaching energetic barriers when held. To touch a Fae with a metal implement isn't about physical pain, but energetic and psychic pain. It allows alien and, in most cases, uncontrolled and unmodified energies to touch them. It also explains why they don't seem to shy away from simple ferrous objects like zips, poppers (snap fasteners in the US), keys, and the like if they are close to our bodies and also why lore is often contradictory, showing the Fae working with and creating ferrous weapons. It is only if we wield them in such a way as to create a conduit that they become a problem. Therefore, it only makes sense that having good psychic and energetic shields is just polite, so don't work with the Fae without making sure both of you are safe and protected with adequate shielding.

THE BLESSINGS OF IVY— A PROTECTION RITUAL

The following ritual builds upon the techniques practiced, creating an excellent daily ritual of purification and protection.

STAGE ONE—THE VERDANT BREATH

Perform the verdant breath exercise as described on page 44. Take your time to get it right. The last thing you want is to start from a weak foundation, so making sure you feel fully cleansed before you start shielding is an absolute must.

STAGE TWO—THE CREEPING SHIELD

As when you were first learning the verdant breath, it can be useful to have an actual plant to work with, as you can study how ivy grows, what the different varieties are, and which one resonates with you the most. Drawing and taking photos might help. This might seem a little extreme, but your personal protection, shielding, and grounding should not be taken lightly. A well-constructed shield maintained daily will last a lifetime.

These steps should follow the verdant breath exercise:

1. Visualize the essence of the ivy reaching out and slowly creeping along your body. Where you start is entirely up to you. Some like to imagine it creeping up from the ground, slowly wrapping around each leg and progressing up their bodies naturally. Others imagine it entering through their crown. You could even start from your nose or elbow, if you want.

2. Keep inhaling and exhaling slowly and consciously. As you do, imagine the plant expanding with each exhalation, growing and feeding on the

carbon dioxide and the waste energy you expel with every breath. Its fine, lacy root structure slowly covers your entire body, creating a barrier. Its rich leaves sprout forth, fed not only by your breath and internal imbalances, but also by anything externally that does not serve your higher good.

3. Once you feel your entire body is adequately covered, hold your breath for a moment. Realize that the tiny roots and suckers are now so deeply connected to you that even a disturbance of a fraction of a millimeter will alert you, both physically and mentally, to what is going on around you as well as absorb any negativity before it becomes part of your own system.

Sit in conscious awareness of your shield for at least seven more breaths before going about your day or settling down to sleep.

STAGE THREE—TWEAKING YOUR SHIELD

The flaw with an all-encompassing shield is that it doesn't really allow for variations in strength or thickness. It is just a one-size-fits-all shield and blocks a large amount of sensory information out. Less than ideal when you consider that there will be times when it's beneficial to change your level of shielding, sometimes shifting the balance to make it a more psychic protection or other times more energetic. You may want to touch something energetically without breaching your general protection, or you may want to suit up so strong mentally that you are donning the psychic equivalent of a tinfoil hat. It will depend on the different people, entities, or situations you are working with. Family and friends probably warrant less shielding. An arrogant boss who shouts and blusters but is essentially all bark will probably leave you feeling battered and bruised but will rarely be a threat to your psyche, whereas certain Fae can make you feel a little dizzy and mentally disoriented. Being able to adjust to those situations will mean that you don't spend a lot of your life feeling like you are operating on mute. So, how do we do it?

Having completed stages one and two and having practiced them enough that you feel you have adequately mastered both, take time to sit enveloped in your beautiful, symbiotic shield of ivy. Feel its delicate, lacelike tendrils covering you. Sense the leaves pulsing in time with your breath, absorbing and oxygenating. Don't rush it. Then, follow the steps below. They should become a regular practice in their own right so as to ensure that you have the skills when the time comes.

1. Imagine that some tendrils are slowly withdrawing, starting at your extremities. Allow them to creep backward up your spine, thickening the growth there. Imagine them spreading up the back of your neck, thickening at the base of your skull and continuing onto the crown of your head and over to your third eye. You soon have a beautiful veil of ivy draped over your head and covering your shoulders. Stay like this for at least seven breaths.

2. When you are ready, let this psychic shield slowly retract, populating your body and extremities again. Let it thicken and grow, covering you from the neck down like the most comforting onesie you've ever slept in, keeping you safe and warm and protected from any energetic rubbish that might end up your way. Stay like this for at least seven breaths.

3. Experiment with different levels of psychic or energetic cover or return to a fully covered shield as practiced in steps 1 and 2, but try to make the cover more or less dense all over.

Play with this. It's actually fun, and when learning is fun, we tend to learn faster and do better. If you can, get another person to play along. See if they can work out what type of shield you are working with, and vice versa. Also, see if you can merge shields. That can be a very effective practice in all kinds of group work.

AND FINALLY—PIMP MY SHIELD

It is possible to work with more than one plant spirit as part of your daily practice, and another plant found very often in urban environments is the dog rose. It is a regular guest in gardens, parklands, and even the large planting pots in city centers. More importantly, dog rose is often found growing in similar locations to ivy. From my experience, the pair seem to work well together.

THE DOG ROSE

The dog rose is a beautiful, delicately fragrant little flower. They grow pretty much anywhere you plant them. They have wicked little spikes that can gash any hand that reaches out too roughly. Dog rose is an excellent addition to anybody's psychic and energetic armor.

As the rose is a symbol of the heart, it's best to plant the core of your dog rose shield directly above the solar plexus. Imagine its delicate petals and pretty yellow stamen. See it trembling slightly with each inhalation and exhalation. Make it as real as possible, and then there it can sit, most of the time just looking very pretty but doing not much more.

When you need a bit of extra something, use the same technique as the ivy blessing. Allow the essence to expand, visualizing just a couple of stems winding around your arms and legs. This is great when entering a potentially difficult situation. At this stage, the dog rose is barely there at all, but should you feel vulnerable or threatened, you can allow it to spread out, creating what can only be described as a psychic barbwired fence.

The dog rose isn't just a defense mechanism. Should you feel you are entering a threatening situation, you may choose to spread out the dog rose and let it flower profusely. It works as quite an effective glamour. Dog roses, after all, are reminiscent of warm sunny afternoons in the summer: insects buzzing, birdsong in hedgerows, peace, quiet, memories of youth. There is nothing quite like appearing innocuous to diffuse a tense situation. And sometimes working with the Fae can feel very tense indeed. An armor that demonstrates your willingness to work creatively with the spirits of various plants and to enter into a discourse while taking precautions can go a long way to alleviate that tension. As a side note, it works on humans, too. Try it next time someone is giving you grief.

PHYSICAL PROTECTION CHARMS AND AMULETS

Although the purpose of this book is primarily to learn how to interact with any urban Fae we meet, it would be remiss not to include a piece on charms and amulets in a chapter that focuses on personal protection. There is probably not a culture in the world that hasn't developed its own set of protective charms and amulets, a lot of them relating to the good folk. In many cultures, children are considered particularly at risk from Fae interference. The concept of the changeling is widespread, along with suggestions as to how they can best be avoided. This normally entails special hats, clothes, or jewelry. Menstruating women are also considered to be not only vulnerable, but also downright unclean and, as a result of this vulnerability, guilty of putting others at risk. Study of common myths and legends can reveal copious examples of when it is a good time to protect yourself against the interest of the faery folk, and although some of the tales stem from an indoctrinated fear, the truth is that working with the Fae is not something to be taken lightly.

When organized religions started to take hold and the good folk became associated with negative forces in the world, our ancestors became preoccupied with doing everything they could to "pray the Fae away." Hagstones, animal teeth, coins, red thread, bundles of herbs, silver charms, and pieces of iron are regularly cited in folklore, grimoires, and other ancient texts as being effective against the Fae, often in combinations held together in a small pouch that could be worn. Certain Arabic cultures will include miniature items like a dagger and a candlestick so that, spiritually, the wearer can fight the djinn and see them coming. The Italians developed the cimaruta charm, which incorporates, among other things, a knife, a key, and some well-known herbs associated with the Fae, such as rue and valerian. We can take a lot from this evidence and use it to our advantage in situations where we may feel genuinely threatened, for urban Fae are not so different from their more rural counterparts or humanity. Not everyone has our best intentions at heart, after all. Although, thanks to increasing reports of Fae who are no longer bothered by iron, it can be argued that, because they are more comfortable with our human-made environment, we have to be a little more thoughtful about what we include in the charms we create and the amulets we empower.

NOISE AND BELLS

Noises really offend many Fae. Bells are considered a particular nuisance. Historically, the Fae have been known to steal bells and even to relocate from their homes as a result of them. Lake ladies (also known as mere-maids after the name given to lakes in the UK and Western Europe) seem to be particularly offended. Both the Rostherne and the Colne mere-maids repeatedly stole the bell from the newly constructed churches in their vicinity.[11] A Colne mere-maid was helpful and offered an alternative location for the church, perhaps

---

11. F. Woods, *Further Legends and Traditions of Cheshire* (Nantwich, UK: Shiva Publishing, 1982), 30.

indicating that, at one point in history, an uneasy truce between Christianity and the Fae was bartered. A Rostherne mere-maid wasn't so accommodating. She dragged the offending bell through a subterranean tunnel from her lake to the sea. It is said that if you listen at the water's edge of the Mere on a full moon, you can hear the bell knelling from beneath the lake. In nearly every county in England, there is a tale of how the Fae detested the sound of bells, particularly church bells, so much that they were forced to relocate.

A very simple protection charm is to thread some small jingle bells onto a red thread and attach it to your bag or coat or even wear it around your neck as an amulet. From personal experience, don't wear this at night. It might seem like a great idea, but it disturbs your sleep every time you roll over.

CLOTHES AND SHOES

There is one problem with working so hard to become sensitive to the spirits of the otherworld, and that is that your down or alone time can reduce quite drastically. Learning to switch off and shield up can be as important as opening yourself up, but this isn't always sufficient, and there will be times when you don't want to be disturbed by the Fae. Traditional tales teach us that wearing items of clothing inside out can be an effective guard against interference from the Fae. No true explanation is given as to why this is the case, but the general consensus is that it confuses the Fae to such an extent that it allows you to get away. This is one of my preferred methods of protection while sleeping; a T-shirt or sock reversed is a very mundane but effective way to keep from being bothered in the night.

There is similar lore surrounding shoes. Have you ever driven down an expressway and seen a single shoe lying on the side of the road? I do all the time; I also try to work out which shoe it is, for a left shoe thrown in a timely manner is said to banish the Fae! My overactive imagination wonders what happens to the shoe once you have thrown it. Does it land there, ready for you to pick it up again, or does it disappear like socks in a washing machine, possibly appearing on the other side of the world? Maybe it's also displaced in time, lying sad and lonely at the side of a busy road. Anyway, bizarre though this snippet of lore might be, it is almost definitely related to the idea that shoes concealed in walls or chimneys of the home can protect against demons, faeries, goblins, and elves. Although, in the case of concealed shoes, it doesn't seem to matter which shoe is concealed, just that it is. There is no definitive reason that historians can find for this, but it seems clear that, much like other apotropaic charms such as witch bottles, there is an intended sympathetic link between the owner of the shoe and the shoe itself.

While I don't advocate throwing your shoes about and running home barefoot on busy town and city streets, using an old and worn shoe as a home protection charm is worth experimenting with. Chimneys and large flags that can be lifted at the main entrance are no longer really a thing, but that doesn't mean we can't place the shoe under a floorboard or in an attic or crawl space. Make sure you ritualize this act. It's not just about shoving an old shoe in an odd location; it's about stating that this shoe represents you, and any harm or foul that might come your way from the supernatural should miss its mark and hit the shoe instead.

WITCH BOTTLES

These amulets take the idea of a sympathetic connection between the maker and the item one step further. They are filled with all manner of goodies, including nail clippings, hair, urine, blood, red thread, bent pins, and crooked nails. The idea is that the bottle is placed at the boundary of the home—normally buried, but some have been found in attics, chimneys, and walls as well. Any Fae, witches, demons, and so on will energetically home in on the bottle, thinking it may be the person they intend to harm. Once they enter the bottle, however, they are impaled upon the bent pins and nails and tangled in the thread, trapping them forever.

In reality, a witch bottle to ward against the Fae isn't normally necessary unless you've done something to really annoy them. Humans are normally the problem, but it's worth discussing, just in case.

GIFTS

Of course, there is the ultimate insult—one that is most present in the public psyche: giving clothing. Thanks to J. K. Rowling and the adorable house elf Dobby, we are all now aware that giving an item of clothing to a domestic helper spirit frees it from servitude. This doesn't just work for a Fae who has been contracted or bound, either; you may have read the story of *The Elves and the Shoemaker* as a child. Two unbound helper spirits just up and leave the minute the shoemaker's wife provides them with clothing. If you have a domestic helper faery whom you would like to gently move on, leaving a small scarf that you have knitted or even a pair of socks is a far nicer way of asking them to leave than banishing them against their will.

However, there are several species of Fae who cannot take direct acknowledgment or thanks for their work. To acknowledge them is to risk extreme ire. It's a tricky situation as other species ask for thanks. The bannick loves to be thanked for their work and considers it only polite.[12] This is where the practice of offerings comes in. It is a way of showing gratitude—honestly a far more genuine act than some empty words, anyway. When you leave items out for the Fae, you can add some words to make it clear that these are, indeed, intended as a form of gratitude. You can make your own words or just use the following:

> *I thank the Mother for her blessings and the help I have received today.*
> *I leave this* [insert offering] *as a sign of my respect.*

12. Psudowolf, "Master of the Bathhouse: Bannick," The Bestiary, accessed October 31, 2019, https://shadowsflyte.wordpress.com/2014/05/18/master-of-the-bathhouse-bannick/.

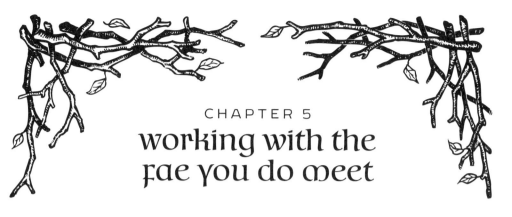

working with the fae you do meet

Take nothing. Eat nothing.
However, if any creature tells you that it hungers, feed it.
If it tells you that it is dirty, clean it.
If it cries to you that it hurts, if you can, ease its pain.[13]

Some of the best and most sustainable daily practices are ones that do not cause inconvenience or negative impact upon our daily lives. We live with our neighbors and work colleagues day in and day out, and while from time to time we may go out of the way to make them feel special, such as throwing a party or bringing a cake into work on a birthday, as a general rule, our interactions are fairly low-key. On the Isle of Man, there is a now-famous bridge known as the Fairy Bridge. People come from across the world to have their photos taken beside the sign. Local buses have an automated announcement system that reminds all passengers that it is custom to greet the faeries, and several urban myths are now circulating that certain local taxi drivers will actually stop their vehicles if their passengers do not greet the otherworldly residents of the bridge appropriately. Failure to do so is said to bring bad luck.

Now, of course, the cynical will say it is a wonderful gimmick thought up by the tourist board. And there's almost definitely a lot of truth in that, but the practice has been in existence for a very long while. As we have already discussed, it's these shreds of lore that show us how we can work reliably with the Fae. A chirpy hello as you pass can often be enough, and it barely takes seconds out of your day. Totally sustainable.

---

13. N. Gaiman and C. Vess, *Instructions* (London: Bloomsbury Publishing, 2010).

Places to acknowledge the Fae include liminal places—alleys, bridges over running water—and always say hello if there is some urban myth or folklore associated with the place. This includes the threshold into your own backyard or home. You are, after all, most likely to have a Fae encounter in your own backyard!

OFFERINGS

One of the best ways of building a relationship with anybody is to treat them well. I know giving offerings as a way of making contact might feel a little like bribing the Fae, but if you consider your own interactions with the people you meet, then you can't help but realize that many friendships start because of mutual self-interest. The relationship often develops as a result of an exchange of time, energy, or even material items. There has been a long history of us providing offerings to the Fae and also of them providing offerings to us.[14]

It is fair to say that the Fae are very fond of offerings. They do see offerings as a mutual exchange—you would like to make contact, and they really want your gifts. These gifts can be material objects, small shiny trinkets, ribbons, stones, leaves, pebbles, promises, and so on. The list is endless. But one thing they enjoy more often than not is food. When comparing modern offerings to those found historically in tales, many stock favorites haven't changed that much, so if you have the time and inclination, you may want to research to find specific offerings local to your area, as they will almost undoubtedly still be current. Being in an urban environment doesn't affect the offering types much, either. I have listed a few of the most common substances and materials below. However, you may find that there are some surprising cautions that go against popular beliefs about the Fae.

BREAD

Reverend Robert Kirk, author of a wonderful book that is a must-read for all Fae workers, claimed that bread, "as human food hateful to Fairies," was used to ward off unwanted attention after childbirth, thus protecting both

---

14. J. Cutchin, *A Trojan Feast: The Food and Drink Offerings of Aliens, Faeries, and Sasquatch* (San Antonio, TX: Anomalist Books, 2015), 91–106.

the mother and the child from changelings. A "stale crust of bread" kept in a pocket is, according to some tales, purported to scare away the Fae.[15]

I've never personally felt any inclination to offer bread on a regular basis, and I've most certainly never been asked for it. However, there are some tales in which the Fae are offered bread and other grain products, such as the tale of the Physicians of Myddfai, where a mere-maiden was enticed to marry a human man with an offering of bread. It is worthy of note that the maiden refuses the bread twice before agreeing to marry the young lad, first because the bread was too hard, second because it was raw. She only succumbs to his charms with an offering of part-baked bread and a heartfelt declaration of his love offering himself to her for eternity.[16]

It's likely that the youth's declaration of undying love was the thing that did the trick, for nowhere does it say that the maiden ever actually ate the bread. Further investigation of bread-related offerings worldwide clearly shows that the act of cooking or processing doesn't affect what is considered offensive either— some French Fae like unprocessed grain, Italian Fae like pasta, the faery threshers of Dartmoor worked for a steady supply of bread and cheese, and the knockers, who can be found in mines all around the world, are often appeased with a piece of pastry. So, it may be fair to say that bread and its acceptability as an offering may be, to some extent, species- and location-specific.

What is it that makes this foodstuff so hateful to certain faeries? So much so that one of the best-known authorities believed the substance to be hateful to the Fae? It's probably a combination of things, such as the aforementioned location and species, but ingredients may also play a very large factor, not least that salt is a vital ingredient to any bread recipe that we would consider palatable. Try making a loaf without it and see what I mean. I contemplated this for some time and have asked several Fae if they would consider bread as a worthy offering, and it was suggested to me that an unsalted, handmade flatbread would be acceptable, especially if it had been infused with herbs that are considered beneficent by the Fae, which in turn would probably make it unfit for human consumption.

15. R. Kirk and A. Lang, *The Secret Commonwealth: Of Elves, Fauns, and Fairies* (Glastonbury, UK: The Lost Library, 1893), xxix–xxx, 13–14.

16. T. Breverton, *The Physicians of Myddfai: Cures and Remedies of the Mediaeval World* (Carmarthenshire, UK: Cambria Books, 2012), part 3.

Despite the fact that history shows that bread is only really received well by certain spirits, so many people leave bread as an offering. I feel there has to be some value to it. We know the Fae have evolved just like us and are just as opportunistic as we are, so it isn't surprising that they might accept an offering that was previously considered unsuitable. However, the one thing I would suggest is that you absolutely don't use processed, packaged supermarket bread. Not only is the salt content very high, but most manufacturers actually fortify their doughs with iron. Poor offerings can cause offense.

· EXERCISE ·
making faery flatbread

This recipe is really easy to make, and the herbs included are ones that you should be able to collect in towns and cities anywhere in Europe and North America. For other locations, you may need to substitute other local herbs. The herbs recommended here are all ones that have known faery connections and the added benefit of being fit for consumption. That way, should an animal or a very desperate human stumble across your offering, you can rest assured that you will not be poisoning them.

Ingredients:

2 cups (300 grams) of plain flour

4 tablespoons (50 grams) of butter

¾ cup (185 milliliters) of milk

Herbs (yarrow, mugwort, and/or clover), chopped—a good pinch of each

Oil for cooking

Heat butter and milk in a pan until the butter has melted, then combine with the flour and herbs to make a soft dough. Sprinkle a little more flour on the work surface and knead for a couple of minutes until the dough is soft and smooth. You can add more flour if the dough is a little too sticky. Let the dough rest in the fridge for at least thirty minutes.

Cut your dough into four and roll each quarter into round balls. These can then be rolled out into rounds; about three millimeters (⅛ inch) is perfect. Heat oil in the pan and cook each side for one to two minutes until the dough bubbles and areas start to brown. When you flip to the second side, press down on the bubbles to help keep them flat and more uniformly cooked.

Once cooked, stack them and drizzle with honey or milk as part of the offering plate, if you wish.

....

ALCOHOL (AND OTHER NONALCOHOLIC LIQUIDS)

Kirk also claimed that fine, spirituous liquors gave nourishment to the Fae. In my experience, that is very true. Dark rums seem to be a popular offering to all kinds of Fae creatures. As is good dark beer, such as a stout, porter, or a black IPA. Home brew is received very well, and the stronger the better. The pechs of Scotland, a particular species of dwarf, were credited with knowing the secret recipe to brewing a most delicious heather beer, and the practice of the brownie stone in Scotland first originated with brewers offering a beer libation to the faeries in return for a swift and successful fermentation process.

Processed prepackaged products don't appear to be an issue here, for which I am very grateful, because I'm a very busy lady, and my brewing skills suck. However, if you'd like to give it a go, I can assure you your offering will be gratefully received with little fuss. One of the nice things about offering alcohol over bread or physical items in an urban location is both the portability and also the absence of long-term physical evidence. A poured libation from a small bottle beside a road or parking lot can disappear in minutes. It's a perfect "opener." Think of it like buying somebody a drink in a bar. You offer the drink; if they accept, then normally a conversation starts. It might just be the equivalent of a bit of banter and chitchat. Don't push it too hard. These things take time. Next time you come along, you will be remembered.

One thing I would like to stress is, please, please, please do not go against either your ethics or your recovery program to offer alcohol. Sobriety is a wonderful gift to be cherished, and nothing should jeopardize that. Even a desire to work with the Fae.

There are other substitutes that can be used. I have happily offered coffee, milk, and fruit juices successfully. Coffee is actually a great one for stealth offerings on busy streets, because nobody thinks twice about somebody taking the lid off their travel cup and pouring out the dregs. They will just walk past you in the street and assume your coffee has gone cold.

MILK

Mixed milk and honey is a particular favorite of various house brownies and other residential spirits, so that can also be offered when out and about. The numerous boggarts who live across the industrial North of England are often a pest or menace because a lazy housekeeper or a forgetful homeowner forgot to leave out a due portion for the spirits in return for their help and support around the home.

In Welsh lore, it is customary to leave either cream or milk upon a doorstep to appease both the Bendith y Mamau and the Wild Hunt, forms of trooping Fae that we will look at in more detail later.

Along with butter and cream, milk is a very affordable, easily obtainable substance. Please be very careful where you leave it, however, as there is an environmental impact with dairy products. Cats, dog, and hedgehogs are all lactose intolerant. I place my dairy offerings in a small earthenware bowl that has a lid, like a mini tagine. If faeries are clever enough to come in and help around the house, they are more than capable of lifting a lid to get their reward.

TOBACCO

As with alcohol, I start this with the caveat that if tobacco causes you any ethical or relapse issues, please don't use it. For many years, this was my go-to offering, as I was a smoker and had a pouch of loose rolling tobacco on my person at all times. It was easy to reach into my pocket and pull a good pinch out, letting it fall from my hands with just a few words of blessing. Like spilled liquids, a small pile of loose tobacco is unlikely to raise any attention. People drop tobacco all the time when they are making their cigarettes. However, once I quit, it took me years before I felt I was able to use it again as an offering without it being a temptation. I now have a tiny pouch of tobacco I carry if I am specifically going out to investigate new areas, and I sometimes burn it on charcoal as an incense, but as a rule, even a decade later, I still don't use it regularly.

Tobacco has a long history of spiritual use. Before it made its way to Europe, it was used by First Nation people for a whole host of different ceremonial purposes, including communication with spirit. I suspect (although proof is impossible) that it was this knowledge brought back from the New World that inspired many other cultures to start using tobacco as an offering. It would have been an expensive substance, and offerings of value are rarely rejected when given with good intent. The Romanians now have a faery or spirit of tobacco and smoking called the pâca, which is an excellent example of a class 3 spirit, a fully adapted and sentient Fae, one that now thrives in the modern world.

Many other cultures also have tales of tobacco. The Irish gruagach was offered a pipe and tobacco to smoke by a young farmhand in the farmhand's quest to marry the king of Ireland's daughter.[17] A whole host of African spirits are seen smoking pipes and are offered tobacco, either through ingestion or as an altar offering. The Filipinos even have a tale of a volcano spirit who presided over an army of dwarfs whose sacred plant was the tobacco, so it's fair to say that it is a substance universally liked by the Fae.

If you would like to try this as an offering without the ethical implications of supporting the tobacco industry, I would wholeheartedly consider planting a tobacco plant. *Nicotiana sylvestris* is a purely ornamental tobacco plant and has the most amazing floral scent, which is an offering in its own right. The plants reach a reasonable height and tend to prefer well-drained herbaceous borders rather than a pot. The flowers do well in vases, and the leaves can be taken to locations to be left. Don't be tempted to scatter the seeds in any location other than your own backyard. There are implications with introducing non-native species, even accidentally. Japanese knotweed, Himalayan balsam, and canary grass are now considered invasive in the UK, having first been introduced by the Victorians into their ornamental gardens. Collecting the seeds at the end of the season and using them sparingly in a faery flatloaf is a good way to make use of this plant as well; just beware. The plant is toxic, so be careful where you leave the offering and how many seeds or leaves you use.

SILVER

With the exception of certain mythological beasts, which are beyond the remit of this book, silver is almost universally considered to be a sacred metal to the Fae. I have gifted actual sterling silver items to the Fae. I have also asked them to take back silver that I have perceived to be tainted magickly by burying it in the ground: I have found more and more that it is the sparkle, the actual metallic shine, that is the biggest attractor of silver. As a rule, I generally find

17. J. Curtin, *Myths and Folk Tales of Ireland* (New York: Dover Publications, 1975).

that pieces of silver are normally requested in quantities of three, five, seven, or nine, depending on the situation. Small denomination "silver" coins work perfectly for this and make this request far more affordable than giving away pieces of precious jewelry.

HONEY AND CANDY

After milk, honey is probably one of the most common offerings found in folkloric documents and fairy tales. In fact, any items that are sweet to taste are, without a doubt, the most successful and popular. When offerings of this type are given as part of a particular piece of ritual work, they almost always herald a positive interaction. It is worth looking into regional delicacies when considering a sweet offering, but don't worry if you don't have any local specialties. Fudge is universally accepted as it consists of foodstuffs that are individually favored by the fair folk: milk, butter, and sugar. What's not to like?

FAERY HERBS

It's long been known and documented in folktales and urban myth that certain herbs and plants are connected with the otherworld:

- Yarrow
- Rue
- Ragwort (St. John's wort)
- Yew
- Mugwort
- Wormwood
- Mistletoe
- Rowan
- Willow
- Hawthorn
- Clover

Some charms suggest that the use of certain herbs, potions, and ointments can be used to aid in gaining "the sight" in order to have closer contact with the faery realms. Due to the nature of the ingredients, it would take at least a year to gather everything needed for the recipe. This is an excellent devotional activity to show your intention to work sincerely with the Fae. Most of these charms suggest anointing your physical eyes with the ointment or potion, but ritually anointing your third eye is very effective and almost definitely safer. As part of a larger ritual, this can add much to your practice.[18]

· EXERCISE ·
making faery anointing water

As with everything in this book, these ingredients can be found in and around urban locations, such as at the edges of parking lots and roadsides or growing as weeds in municipal flower beds or common land. They can also be purchased online. If you intend to gather or grow these ingredients, then this recipe is best started at Samhain as it will take approximately a year to complete.

Ingredients:

Spring water (for the elixir and to create faery bathing water)

Rose petals

Marigold petals

Hazel buds (ground up nuts will do if you can't find a hazel tree)

Thyme (flowers or new growth)

Hollyhock flowers

Olive oil

METHOD

The first step is to make faery bathing water. This is reasonably simple to do. Take a deep bowl filled with gently warmed spring water (bottled will do, but if you fancy making a trip to a special location containing a spring or well, even better) along with a small piece of soap and a towel. Place these out where you believe the Fae frequent. You can use any portal location (see Journeying and Scrying on page 87) or your back garden. Old charms suggested that the purpose of this water was to collect the scum from the top of the water after the faeries had bathed. Obviously, essence of grubby faery is the important part of this recipe.

---

18. K. Briggs, "Some Seventeenth-Century Books of Magic," JSTOR, Accessed November 20, 2019, https://www.jstor.org/stable/1257871?origin=JSTOR-pdf&seq=1.

Clear winter nights during a full moon are an ideal time to collect the faery bathing water. A frost will freeze the top layer of the water, allowing you to skim off the frozen top, thus concentrating the solution. Only a few drops are necessary for the rest of this recipe. Any surplus can be bottled to create an additional elixir at your leisure.

On a Wednesday, combine one part olive oil with three parts spring water and seven drops of faery bathing water. If you have purchased or already possess the other botanical ingredients, now is the time to add them. Shake the mixture thoroughly each morning and evening for at least a month, allowing the ingredients to thoroughly infuse. If you intend to add the botanicals as they come into season as part of a long devotional activity, store the base liquid containing the oil, spring water, and faery bathing essence in a sealed container in a cool, dry location until the ingredients are ready. In this case, leave the mixture for at least another month after the final ingredient has been added to ensure that it has infused well. Finally, strain and put the mixture into a brown glass bottle. Use sparingly to anoint your third eye.

Note: You don't need gallons of this elixir, but your bottle needs to be big enough to include the botanicals. A nine-ounce bottle will more than suffice.

ACCEPTING FOOD—A FINAL WARNING

When the Greek god Hades stole the goddess Persephone and took her to the underworld, he tricked her into eating just three pomegranate seeds. From that point forward, the goddess was destined to spend a portion of each year with him in the underworld, unable to return home permanently to her mother's side. In another tale, Childe Rowland was urged by Merlin not to "bite no bit, and drink no drop, however hungry or thirsty you are" while he searched Elphame for his sister, who had, for reasons unknown to us, run widdershins around the church and been abducted by faeries.[19] These examples are just two of quite literally hundreds of a protagonist or hero being warned against eating food in the otherlands. While our food seems to be perfectly acceptable to the Fae, the same cannot be said for theirs.

During all scrying, journeying, trance walking, or other altered states, should you find yourself being offered food, do not accept it. I cannot tell you

---

19. J. Jacobs, *English Fairy Tales* (Overland Park, KS: Digireads, 2011), 77.

what would happen if you did, but the sheer weight of anecdotal evidence suggests that absolutely no good will come of it. That being said, should you have the good fortune of witnessing a full manifestation in this world and they offer you food, then there is no reason not to take it. The problem seems to lie in eating their food in the otherworld only.

SAYING HELLO

I remember very clearly on two occasions people crowing smugly that I had not been able to enter their homes until I had been invited. They attributed this to their superior wards and protection spells. This irritated me greatly. I found the comments foolish and still do. I didn't enter their home because I was brought up well, and one of the manners taught to me in my childhood was not to enter someone's home unless invited. Likewise, unless I expressly invite people to enter my home freely at any time, I expect the same behavior in return.

It can, of course, be argued that the wards picked up some ill desire on my behalf, causing my ingrained politeness to kick in. Well, if those were my wards, I really wouldn't be telling the person who triggered them that the wards were in place. Would you? You'd just be looking for trouble to come and tamper with them. Suffice to say that in both situations, my desire to visit and extend the friendship had lessened. Beware those who cannot even hold to one of the four basic foundations of magick when it comes to their own protection: to keep silent. They may well have problems keeping silent about other things, too!

These experiences provide some interesting food for thought. Politeness is very important to the Fae. More than one or two folktales and stories tell of humans unwittingly offending the Fae through a lack of politeness and protocol and then suffering their wrath. The desire for good manners has not changed with the evolution of the urban Fae. And although they are far more tolerant than their country kin, I generally believe that a little bit of courtesy and respect goes a very long way.

MAKING INTRODUCTIONS

We have already talked in some depth in chapter 1 about the importance of learning the name of the Fae you choose to work with. This may happen very quickly or take months; you may also never learn the name at all, depending on the nature of Fae you are working with.

Contact with the Fae is not just about knowing the name, though. It's also about how you introduce yourself, how you ask for things, and how you show your connections and ties to other beings. Just like humans, the Fae are both nepotists and social climbers. Knowing somebody more powerful and dropping a name can often take you a long way. The age-old story of not what you know, but who you know.

SO HOW DO YOU DO IT?

In my experience, it's all rather formal. The Fae love connections, affiliations, and lineages. When the time is right, start with your full name, who your father and mother are, what your magickal affiliations are, and so on. I would be wary of giving this information unless you have built a relationship; blurting this out too soon may put you at a disadvantage.

Once you have identified potential locations and spirits, it's important to realize that there are polite ways of initiating contact and introducing yourself. So many mistakes are made by well-intentioned blundering. You wouldn't meet someone while out for a walk, have a short chat, and then follow them home, let alone walk into their lounge and put your feet up on their coffee table, now would you? Of course not. That kind of behavior would find you making friends with local law enforcement rather than getting to know your fellow walker.

Relationships in our reality are built slowly. We are creatures of instinct, and, as a rule, we are slow to trust. We are often drawn inexplicably to those who fascinate us, and sometimes there is no rhyme or reason to this attraction. Meanwhile, other people leave us cold. I have lived in my current location for over three years now, and I walk my dog through the same streets and common land on a daily basis. I regularly run into the same people over and over. Some are now on a first-name basis, their dogs and mine running around our feet as we amble along, chatting about minor things. Others I barely make eye contact with, even if I see them more regularly.

It's the same with Fae. Once you are sure there is something there, don't go rushing headlong in. Take time to walk that area daily. Just as we are mostly oblivious to the people we share space with on our daily commute to work, the spirits of the otherworld are mostly oblivious to us and our comings and goings. We are no more consequential to them than a beetle is to us. But they are very quick to pick up when someone notices them. Therefore, a gentle nod is going to be more than enough to get their attention. Do this if it feels right; keep your head down and move along if it doesn't.

For every faery I have worked with, I have probably quietly passed a dozen by. Not every Fae wants to interact with us. Perhaps they are too busy, on an important errand, late for an appointment, or just don't like the feel of us. The reasons are not important, but without fail, the energy they will project when they don't want to make contact will feel the same, almost malefic. At times, this sensation can be downright terrifying. I strongly urge you to pay attention to this sensation when you come across it and to do your daily practical exercises to ensure your psychic senses are honed and your shields are maintained. They will keep you safe and ensure no offense is given.

THE POWER OF NAMES

Some legends tell that the creatures of the faery realms can take great offense at being addressed directly, so our ancestors came up with a whole host of names by which to address them indirectly. Use these names when first interacting with the entities you encounter. Once you have established a rapport, more personal names may be shared:

- The kindly ones
- The spirits
- The sídhe
- The Fae/faery
- The good neighbors
- The good people
- The good crowd
- The honest folk
- The fair folk
- The little people
- The seelie and unseelie ones
- The Mother's blessings

There are other more specific names, such as gnome, pixie, elf, dryad, and so on, but as some of these names are location-specific, and as the lines between each cultural group can be very blurred, it isn't helpful to use these names to start with. So, stick to something nice and generic.

Once I am sure that I am in a place frequented by the Fae, I stop for just a moment every time I visit and quietly acknowledge their presence. I know it can be daunting to start speaking to yourself on a busy street, but the reality is we are all so caught up with our own worlds that nobody notices. And those few keen-eyed folk who do are so conditioned to not react to anything out of the ordinary that they are likely to just quietly move away, assuming you are speaking on a phone using an earbud. It does get a little more complicated when you are trying to interact on a deeper level, particularly if you are asked to leave offerings in return for favors, but for now, don't worry too much about that. Where there is a will, there is always a way.

I normally start simple. I take a few moments for rhythmic breathing, focus both my mundane and psychic vision to the area where I perceive the faery to be, and ask the spirit how they are.

Good morning, fair one(s). How goes it with you on this day.
May the blessings of the Mother be with you.

Although it is possible you will get a reaction immediately, it may also be weeks or even months before you get a response. If what you are contacting is a class 1 or 2 spirit, they may be confused by their location and circumstance and also because someone is interacting with them. Remember, these beings will take more work, so be patient. It's worth it in the long run.

Perseverance and an honest and genuine heart are the keys here. If you go into this work with those two attributes, then it is likely that you are going to end up having a meaningful interaction. As discussed earlier, knowing the name of a Fae creature can be very powerful indeed. Once you feel ready to move to the next level, you may wish to consider any one of the calls discussed in the next section on invocation. These have all come from established folklore, and although you shouldn't believe everything you read, there is always a grain of truth in every tale. But for now, just slowly build a relationship and nurture it as if you were nurturing a new friendship.

DON'T FORGET THE FAERY FIELD JOURNAL

Take a notebook out with you on your investigations and continue to dowse the area over a period of time. What you find may not be the "home" of the beings you are sensing, but merely a passing place. You could find that you see, feel, or hear different things at different times of day.

Write down everything you experience. Something that may appear inconsequential could be part of a pattern that allows you to understand who and what you are dealing with. For example, the feeling of dread when you walk down the alley with the empty dumpsters may be far stronger on a Wednesday morning. Why is this? Have the binmen recently disturbed the area again, unsettling something barely conscious of what is going on? Consider those possibilities. It might be best to make contact with this creature when it is less at odds and confused.

Plant divas can definitely be interesting creatures to work with, so, even if you are in the most urbanized of places, take note of the flora and fauna. Plants such as ivy, dog rose, mugwort, agrimony, and scarlet pimpernel flourish in wasteland environments. And don't forget to take notes on other mundane energies. It has been stated that in the UK, you are never more than twenty feet away from a rat, so try to get a feel for the energy of the wildlife and humans who are also sharing your space. Get to know this place like the back of your hand, and just allow those early tentative smiles. Acknowledge each other when your realities collide and you become mutually aware of each other's presence. And if the time feels right, introduce yourself formally.

SIGNS AND SYMBOLS

Not all encounters will result in physical manifestation. Not all of us have true sight. But there are often other signs that indicate your attempts to communicate have been successful. For example, an acquaintance has reported to me that after a successful encounter, they regularly find playing cards lying on the sidewalk. Other phenomena may include things that you thought were lost forever reappearing in unusual places, close calls where you got off lightly, and auditory or visual anomalies.

Fae are often quite shy. Many will not appear directly to even the most psychic of humans, preferring instead to manifest at the corner of your vision. When this happens, it's best not to move or turn your head, no matter how much you want to. And you will want to. We have evolved as predators, and so it is our knee-jerk reaction to want to face anything we catch in our peripheral vision head-on. It goes against every ounce of our being to let something creep up beside us, but this is by far the most effective way of making regular visual contact with any spirit. It will also ensure that certain Fae who don't like being seen aren't chased away permanently or, worse still, leave you suddenly unable to use your "sight" in that location; history is full of tales in which Fae physically remove someone's ability to see them if they are found out.

If you've been practicing your hagstone exercises, then defocusing your eyes even without a stone can be a really good way of beating the urge to turn your head and slowly achieving a direct vision. Quick head movements will cause most spirits to withdraw, so don't do it. I know this is starting to sound like a cracked record, but nothing about building a lasting and safe relationship with the Fae is quick. Should you find yourself in the lucky situation of seeing one of the good folk directly, then the general advice is not to let them out of your sight. Now, this doesn't mean that you can't blink; damage due to dry eyes is not the desired end result. But without fail, the Fae in question, unless they want you to see them, will do anything they can to break the contact, so be wise to any tricks they may play to make you look away long enough for them to escape.

Animals appearing is also a good sign that you have made a successful connection, particularly if those animals act in an atypical way. I've been startled regularly by badgers and hedgehogs in inner-city locations. On its own, this isn't really much, as habitat loss in the UK means that, much like the Fae, we are seeing more rural animals wandering our streets after dark. It is the type of encounter that makes it a "tell." As a rule, hedgehogs don't come willingly and sit in your lap while you are meditating, and badgers, who have notoriously poor eyesight, tend to bolt at the first whiff of a human and rarely choose to accompany you as you walk through deserted streets until you acknowledge them and wish them good night!

We get so engrossed in looking for external validation that it's easy to forget there are other ways of validating a contact. Physiological responses are also an excellent tell. The obvious ones are hairs rising on the back of the neck, goose bumps, rapid temperature changes, and inexplicably feeling panicked or out of breath. In Saxon and Germanic folklore, hiccups and nightmares were always caused by elves. My personal experience aligns with this belief. In a recent talk I gave at a camp where people were mildly mocking the idea of such phenomena, a rather large and butch gentleman suddenly let out the loudest hiccup I had ever heard. The group became very silent very quickly, much to my amusement, and the gentleman in question poured the remains of his coffee in libation at the door of the activities tent as he left.

Other mythologies suggest that knotted hair is also a sign that you have made contact. The sídhe in Irish mythology were known for tangling, plaiting, and knotting hair. Other spirits elsewhere in the world demonstrate their presence by unknotting complex cornrows with a single touch. Although a fairly widespread phenomenon, to use it as a reliable verification of contact is very hit-or-miss, especially if you have a lot of hair or no hair at all. But bear it in mind when investigating new areas—it might be the clue that you need.

Also, plaiting hair can be quite an interesting way to invoke certain Fae. Plaiting and knotting have been associated with magick since the ancient Egyptians. Threads of various colors were used to achieve any number of desired outcomes. Red thread has long been associated with the Fae. Consider creating a braid tied with red ribbon or thread before you head out on your adventures. A small braid at the nape of the neck that you can touch is an excellent trigger to allow your brain to realize that certain energetic work is about to begin or end.

WHAT HAPPENS WHEN THEY WON'T WORK WITH YOU?

It's worth repeating multiple times: the good folk take offense really easily! Inappropriate offerings such as clothes can cause a faery to leave and never return. Offended house brownies will happily transform into a boggart if you regularly leave a mess—brownies really hate messes. And may all the gods bless you if you do something as foolish as thank them for their help. Feral Fae who have started adapting are less sensitive, but not by much, so it's best to treat them as you would their rural cousins.

If you have sensed a Fae but you are getting no obvious response, it is possible that they are offended. It may not have been you who caused the offense, but as the human attempting to make contact, you will be held accountable for the slight. Fae are like us; they have unique and individual personalities, and they can have a bad day, week, or year the same way we do (although in their case, it might be a bad millennium—these folk do hold grudges). Your ability to make recompense for any situation is going to come down to how the Fae feels on the day you make contact. There are some things that can be done, but this normally requires the Fae in question being seelie and willing to tell you what you need to do.

If they won't interact with you at all, you can try regular and unconditional offerings in the hopes of bribing them into communication. Sadly, you cannot in any way guarantee that your offering will be accepted, so you could waste months or years in this attempt at reconciliation. If you decide to go down this route, set a deadline of a month or two at most of regular propitiation; after this time, if you have made no progress, then walk away and leave it, at least for a while. Maybe until you have contact with other local and more powerful Fae who might intercede on your behalf.

One thing I ask myself in both mundane and magickal relationships is, "Why do I need to have an interaction with this being?" If there isn't a good reason, why are you flogging a dead horse? Fae aren't that scarce when you know where to look; there are plenty more mere-maids in the canal.

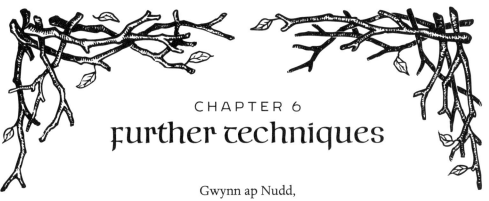

ƒurther techniques

Gwynn ap Nudd,
you who are yonder in the forest,
for the love of your mate,
permit us to enter your dwelling.[20]

A lot of the focus so far has been on how to classify the Fae, what tools to use, what mental and psychic skills you need to develop to achieve the best results, and ways of protecting yourself. But what is it all for? While having a nice introduction and giving gifts can be an awful lot of fun, just acknowledging a faery with no real intent or guarantee that they will show will wear thin quickly. In this chapter, we will look at how to reliably call upon our faery friends once we know where they are (and they us), and we will learn a little bit about exploring the world of Faerie.

CHANTS AND INVOCATIONS FROM HISTORY

When I was first researching the historical techniques of faery invocation, I was surprised by the extent of folkloric information available. There are some really excellent chants and phrases and even whole rituals in certain grimoires. Canting, or chanting, is common among many types of faeries found worldwide. Remember how the queen discovered Rumpelstiltskin dancing and chanting around his fire.

A strong rhyme with a good rhythm not easily broken can be all you need to make a successful, reliable connection. I am very keen on creating my own

---

20. C. Lindahl, J. McNamara, and J. Lindow, *Medieval Folklore: A Guide to Myths, Legends, Tales, Beliefs, and Customs* (New York: Oxford University Press, 2002).

charms, spells, and invocations; however, inspiration can be obtained from lore and should not be ignored. These stories and rhymes have persisted for a reason: they work!

The chant listed below was found in a small regional magazine in the UK. It's from the 1950s, showing that, until very recently, our parents and grandparents were still aware of the Fae and possibly using this kind of chant or prayer in everyday rural life. You may recognize it; I use an adaptation of it to help induce a trancelike state when working with hagstones and also as a mantra during rhythmic walking.

Come in the stillness, Come in the night, Come soon, And bring delight. Beckoning, beckoning, Left hand and right, Come now, Ah, come to-night! [21]

You will note that I substitute "come in the night." Much lore surrounds the nocturnal nature of faeries, almost to the point that it seems the only time you can contact them is nefariously at midnight. This is far from the truth. Many Fae can be found at all times of the day and night. This fascination with nighttime has undoubtedly happened because we are more receptive during these hours, often dozing in hypnogogic states where we see the otherworld far more easily.

Another well-documented nighttime invocation is that of Anne Jeffries, a young Cornish maid who was said to summon the good folk with the following chant:

Fairy Fair and Fairy Bright, come and be my chosen sprite. [22]

In some tales, it was said that she called the name of her faery three times. In another telling, she also performed this ritual on a full moon, adding the following (there is an element of romance about the latter line, but the Fae do like a bit of flattery, so there may be some provenance to it):

Moon shine bright, water's run clear, I am here, but where's my fairy dear? [23]

---

21. Sussex Archeology & Folklore, "Fairy Folklore," Sussex Archeology & Folklore, accessed November 10, 2019, http://www.sussexarch.org.uk/saaf/fairies.html.

22. L. Cooper, *The Element Encyclopedia of Fairies: An A-Z of Fairies, Pixies, and Other Fantastical Creatures* (Falkirk, Scotland: Harper Element, 2014), 165.

23. Ibid., 166.

The spirits of the world of Fae are not and have not been just the remit of the poorly educated and superstitious. Cunning folk and grimoire magicians were and still are rather fixated on them. For example, *The Grimoire of Arthur Gauntlett* and *The Book of Oberon* both contain charms relating to seven faery sisters who can provide the conjurer with anything from treasure to sexual favors. Curiously, another medieval manuscript known as the *Tractatus de Nigromatia* lists a different set of names from the other two grimoires, which may well lend credence to the idea of seelie and unseelie courts. The charm below is taken from *The Grimoire of Arthur Gauntlett*, and the names listed can be used both as an invocatory chant and as part of a purification rite to aid in improving your sight.

Mix well together with a slice of Bay tree upon the palm of thy hand clean washed with Rose water, saying in the tempering of them these words: Julia, Hodelsa, Inafula, Sedamylia, Rouaria, Sagamex, Delforia.[24]

The sixteenth-century German charm listed below introduces the concept of barbarous names and was chanted at the end of a summoning charm intended to call an elf or a dwarf. These are essentially meaningless names used in historical charms, prayers, and spells. They may once have had a meaning to the conjurer, but these meanings have been lost in the mists of time. However, several philosophers and magicians have suggested that it is not the words themselves that have power, but the act of chanting them.

Büma, Lasa, Lamina, Yoth, Athana.[25]

When you are working, there is a lot of worth in chanting freely, allowing sound, no matter how nonsensical, to just flow. You may find a series of words or sounds will start to repeat themselves. Unless the Fae tells you otherwise, include these in any evocation to call them. Spending time researching the words and analyzing them may also give you some indication as to the true name or nature of the Fae you are communicating with.

---

24. D. Rankine, *The Grimoire of Arthur Gauntlet: A 17th Century London Cunning-man's Book of Charms, Conjurations and Prayers* (London: Avalonia Books, 2011), 292–293.

25. C. Lecouteux, *Dictionary of Ancient Magic Words and Spells: From Abraxas to Zoar* (Rochester, VT: Inner Traditions, 2015), 78.

Nursery rhymes and local songs can also be employed in your work when creating invocations. The following are all Old English or Irish rhymes that appear to have some reference to the Fae and could be adapted. The first is a counting rhyme from the county of Norfolk, and it is one of several found across the country that refer to a "little old man." The second rhyme comes from the border county of Shropshire and quite possibly refers to Faery Queen Rhiannon, who was said to ride a milk-white steed dressed in fine gold brocade; this rhyme was considered a precursor to various games, a bit like the rhyme "boys and girls come out to play." Finally, we have a singing rhyme from my own childhood that has a strong feeling of faery about it.

Onery, Twoery, Ickery Am, Bobtail, Vinegar, Tittle and Tam, Harum, Scarum, Madgerum, Marum, Get you out you little Old Man.[26]

A girdle of Gold, a saddle of silk, a horse for me as white as milk.[27]

In and out the dusty bluebells, in and out the dusty bluebells, in and out the dusty bluebells, early in the morning. Tippy tippy tapper tapper on my shoulder, tippy tippy tapper tapper on my shoulder, tippy tippy tapper tapper on my shoulder, early in the morning.

Fairy tales that have survived into the modern day on the whole tend not to include excessive dialog. This doesn't mean that the tales are useless to us; it just serves to prove that when it comes to the Fae, nonverbal communication can be very powerful, for the deeds have survived, if not the actual word. So remember, even if all words fail you, the inhabitants of the otherworld of all types relate well to sympathetic actions, visualizations, movement, music, and physical offerings. You don't need a singing voice or the inspiration of a Celtic bard to get your point across.

· EXERCISE ·
ınvokıng the essence of the ɢenıus loci
Sometimes understanding the energy of a place can really tune you in to the beings who live within or use that space. A fairly safe invocation to practice

---

26. G. F. Northall, *English Folk Rhymes 1892* (India: Vjj Publishing, 2019).
27. Ibid.

is that of the essence of the genius loci. Working with the spirit of any place will also show the residents of Faerie that you aren't just some bumbling oaf, but someone who has taken the time to attune yourself with the landscape around you. Don't skip this one; it will save you from spending hours of time accidentally trying to connect with the local rat colony or the hedgehog under the porch.

This is best practiced at home or in a safe location with a friend or loved one standing guard, as you are going to allow the energy of the spirit of place to get up close and personal. This is going to leave you a little spacey, because your whole body and mind will process a lot of external data that is not your own. The point of this exercise is not to turn inward and focus on a single point, but to expand outward, allowing your locale to become one with you— every noise, movement, and gust of wind; total and utter awareness of the outside world for as far as you can stretch. To become all things at the same time.

Start by finding a comfortable sitting position. You could lie down, but more often than not this can lead to dozing off, so it's not recommended. Run through your rhythmic breathing and also the third eye opening meditation to get you all aligned and mentally receptive to the subtle energies around you. Start with your hearing. Allow your hearing to stretch out. What is the nearest thing you can hear, and what is the farthest? Feel the floor beneath you, the clothes touching your skin, the heat or cold pressing against your exposed areas. Let your ability to feel stretch out farther—to the furniture in the room, the walls, the buildings that surround you. How far out can you go? What else can you feel when you are doing this? Can you feel other people in the buildings? Are there any animals moving around?

If things become overwhelming, draw back a little until there is just enough sensory information there to cope with, and start exploring it. Does it smell? Do you associate colors with it? Are other images coming through that may be a message from the spirit of place? Take your time, but when you feel ready, reverse the process and bring your senses back into yourself: your skin, your breathing, your heartbeat, and so on. Document what you have experienced.

SEALS, SIGILS, AND OTHER CHARMS

In historical literature, we find one or two common behaviors that further back up the idea that evocation of the Fae can be symbolic and nonverbal. After rituals with stones, twig charms are very common. The following charm has been adapted from a charm found in the early nineteenth century; however, it is almost definitely based on a practice known as early as the fifteenth century. In the charm's original form, it was necessary to know the name of the Fae or spirit you wanted to connect with, which, as we know, isn't always possible, particularly with the class 2 and 3 spirits.

· EXERCISE ·

the faery throne charm

This is called the faery throne charm because in its original form, the magician claimed that it was necessary to take hazel twigs to a "faery throne." These thrones are normally tumuli and dolmen found out in the countryside and are often considered places where the Fae reside under the earth or access points to the kingdom of the Fae. Our faery thrones are not quite so glamorous in urban environments. We take them where we can find them, so the spell has been adapted to modern living.

Peel three hazel twigs and flatten them on one side. A lot of councils plant hazel to create decorative foliage in towns and cities, but it is rarely allowed to grow large enough that flattening one side for the purpose of writing on it is going to be easy. Therefore, another option is to use wooden Popsicle sticks. These are easy to get in craft stores and online. They are almost always made of birch, a fast-growing softwood, so if one does go astray, it is fully biodegradable and also less likely to attract unwanted attention, because people will think that it's just litter. It won't be, of course, as you will remove them when you're done, but you don't need to be told that, do you?

On the flat side, write the name of the spirit if you know it, or else give the Fae a generic title. For example, "generous spirit of wood." This is where doing some local research pays dividends, as it will enlighten information like old street names, ghost stories, and even fairy tales that can help you.

On a Wednesday, take three twigs to wherever you think the spirit you want to contact resides, and leave them there, not looking back. The original charm calls for the sticks to be buried, but, as I am sure you can imagine, that makes things a little problematic. If you can cover them or pop them down in the least conspicuous place you can, that is perfect.

Return two days later on Friday during the hours of 8:00, 3:00, or 10:00 (morning or night, but please be safe). If where you left the twigs was a very busy urban environment, it's possible that some of the twigs may have moved or disappeared completely. Take a while to see if you can find them. If all the twigs are moved from the location or gone completely, take this as a sign that the Fae you are trying to contact is not ready to communicate with you at this time. Thank them and depart, doing nothing more.

If all the twigs remain, that is a surefire sign they want to talk. If just one or two remain or they are scattered, it may mean that you are going to have to work a little harder to gain trust, or that your choice of location is a little off. Take time to look around to see if anything jumps out at you. Let your intuition guide you.

If the signs are favorable, call the spirit three times, asking them to appear to you in whatever manner they see fit.

JOURNEYING AND SCRYING

If the old tales are to be believed (and I do believe), it is entirely possible to physically enter the realm of the Fae. Tales from all over the world tell of wells, rivers, caves, and hills where entrances to the realms of the fair folk can be found. You could, in theory, go seek out one of these locations if you really want to, but generally in life, discretion is the better part of valor, and some techniques are more advisable than others. Traveling physically to Faerie is not a reliable technique, as there are far too many potential implications. For example, one of the most common recurring themes in fairy tales is that of the lonely traveler on a remote road late at night who, upon seeing strange lights in the distance, detours off the relative safety of their path only to see beautiful beings dancing within a stone circle or earthwork. Entranced, the traveler dances the night away in gay abandon, neither hungering nor thirsting, but eventually a desire to return home overtakes the traveler, and they ask to leave. In many cases, they return to discover that huge periods of time have passed. All that they know and love has gone, and they are often resigned to a fate of being called a lunatic or fool, for rarely do people believe you when you claim to be someone who should be dead and gone and, worse, who has returned from the otherworld. And sadly, in our current society, little white jackets would definitely be in your future.

In some very rare cases, a warning of this outcome is given by the Fae in an attempt to save the poor soul's life. One very famous story is that Oisin, a Celtic prince whose father, Fionn mac Cumhaill, was the fearsome warrior of the Fianna. Oisin traveled beyond the ninth wave to the Tír na nÓg, the land of the young, where he ruled with the beautiful Faery Princess Niamh at his side. The days were warm and long, the food exquisite, and the wine sweet; he wanted for nothing. But he started to pine and longed to see his homeland; no amount of coaxing by his beautiful bride could persuade him against his plan to return. Eventually, she agreed to lend him her magickal horse so that he could return, but she warned him that if he were to dismount or in any way touch the earth while he was there, he would feel the weight of all the years that had passed while he was in Tír na nÓg, and he would not be able to return.

The young prince set out across the waves and eventually came upon his home in Ireland, but it soon became obvious that it was not the place he had left behind. His father, friends, and sons were all long departed from the world, and men were not the strong, fearsome creatures they had once been. He watched a group of men attempting to move a large boulder in a field, something that he could easily move by himself, so he rode up and leaned over to lift the rock. The strap on his saddle broke, and he tumbled to earth. Within seconds of hitting the ground, he started to age most dramatically, for three hundred years had passed in what had only seemed to Oisin as the blinking of an eye. Astounded, the people called for the holy man whom we now know as Saint Patrick. He took Oisin in and cared for him until he passed away. In those few days, Oisin told many tales of the Fianna and Tír na nÓg, and Saint Patrick wrote them down. It is said that this is the reason we know of the heroic deeds of the Fianna today.

These stories, although prolific, are very extreme, and it is this extremity that has made them worthy of retelling, but the likelihood of this happening to you is infinitesimal. There is also a large amount of metaphor in these tales—a caution to beware losing ourselves in the faery realm, to remind ourselves to stay grounded, and to not forget the physical world around us while questing for the other. I have seen so many seekers of the Fae who—rather than stand one foot firmly in this realm, one foot in the other—have internally crossed so completely that their grip on reality has become tenuous at best and downright delusional at worst. They withdraw from their communities, preferring to spend time alone with their thoughts and the Fae, so enraptured by faery magick that they are mostly oblivious to what is going on around them. When they do eventually return, many of their friends and family have moved on with their lives, leaving the person bereft and alone. They may not have physically entered a ring and returned years later, but they may as well have!

With that word of caution ringing in our ears, if we wish to encounter the Fae in our hometowns and city streets, it's probably best to discuss the possible ways we can enter the faery realms safely and what we can do while we are there.

Two of the safest and most reliable ways of making contact are through the medium of scrying and journeying. These skills can be quickly and easily learned, although they do take a lifetime to master, so be prepared to practice a lot if you want good results.

In addition to these skills, which can quite literally be practiced anywhere, there are points or nodes—essentially little hot spots—that can augment your work, giving it a boost and making the crossing and visions you see far easier and richer. Three of the most common are listed below:

1. The faery ring
2. The thorn gate
3. Portal image

At first glance, the faery ring and thorn gate would seem very historically traditional and rural, but in both instances, they are still quite readily in existence and often within urban or at least suburban locations.

THE FAERY RING

The most common ring available, even in urban environments, is the mushroom ring. Anywhere that grass has been laid, particularly if that grass has been turfed rather than grown from seed, can host such a ring. It takes only a tiny speck of fungal mycelia for rings to grow, and they can be very hard to get rid of. Stories of faery rings are prolific, almost definitely due to the entheogenic nature of the most common species known to create circles. The Celtic folklorist John Rhys also believed that any ring or circle in the grass that was greener than the grass surrounding it was a place in which Bendith y Mamau (Mother's blessings) used to meet to sing and dance.

One of the nice things about using a faery ring as an access point is that there is historical evidence of a built-in fail-safe if you find yourself in an uncomfortable situation. It is widely reported that running around a faery ring nine times can either release you from its thrall or banish the Fae within the circle. Either is likely to get you back in your body and away from any perceived danger. If you feel you are too far away with the faeries, then making yourself get up and move and letting the blood pump and a little bit of adrenalin take hold will ground you out nicely, allowing you to safely return to the here and now.

Stone circles are another form of faery ring sometimes found in older tales. But today, these do not need to be fantastical ancient monuments. Modern stone circles can often be very potent when working with the more adapted Fae, as it is not so much the space itself as the landscape and the circular nature of the construction. In the UK and some other parts of the world, councils and city planning departments are rather fond of sticking random stone circles in roundabouts, shopping malls, and housing estates as forms of artwork, but as with graffiti, there is definitely some Fae interference happening here, because why else would anybody harbor a desire to stick large lumps of stone in random places and call it artwork?

Should you fail to find a naturally occurring space, you can create your own faery ring. It could be inscribed with flowers, chalk, or cornmeal on a floor if you need it to be temporary; however, if you are lucky enough to have a private outdoor space, you could create your own permanent ring with pea gravel, paving flags, stones, or plants. If you do it carefully, the neighbors will think it is decorative.

· EXERCISE ·
entering the faery ring

It would be wise to start your work with the faery ring on either a full or a new moon, both of which are times often associated with the spirits manifesting into this world and portals opening. While historically there may have been some connection with entheogens, a careful examination of these stories show that some of the main protagonists end up in a less-than-desirable situation as a result of eating and drinking and being merry, so go into this exercise stone-cold sober. The only mind-altering substance you should be imbibing in is naturally occurring endorphins, which are easily manufactured through breathing and meditation.

If you can visit an actual faery ring, then please do so. Walk slowly around the circle nine times anticlockwise (widdershins) before stepping into the circle and settling into a comfortable seated position. Using the techniques covered so far, allow yourself to slip into a gentle trance. Chant gently should you wish to, and drum and rattle if you are in a location where it is safe to do so. Allow your mind to drift, to sense, to feel, and maybe even to interact with whoever comes along. When you are ready to leave, thank any being you have been interacting with, and very deliberately remove an item of clothing, reverse it, and place it back on your body. Step out of the ring and return to the here and now by walking nine times around the ring in a deasil (clockwise) manner.

If you are unable to visit an actual ring for health or safety reasons, you can create a ring of your own with thought and care. Crystals, flowers, stone, and feathers gathered and placed in a circle can become your own temporary faery ring, and unlike mushroom rings, which are often season-dependent, you may work with this all year round whenever you please.

THE THORN GATE

I first became aware of the power of the thorn gate through two fellow occultists. Having been drawn to an almost matching pair of hawthorn trees isolated in the landscape, they were fascinated to discover mistletoe growing in the branches. While it is not unusual for this parasitic plant associated with both the Fae and the Druids to grow in hawthorn, hawthorn isn't its first choice either, and this piqued an interest. Also, these particular trees appeared to have a track to nowhere running through them, and they had a stronger energetic hum than the usual background buzz associated with such trees.

After several moonlit nights during which they made offerings to the trees to reveal their secrets and the source of the added energy, they were given a very clear vision of the sunrise aligning with the gap within the trees on the equinoxes. Then, appearing as if from a mist, either the seelie or the unseelie court came trooping across an almost invisible boundary that shimmered between the trees. The other court shortly followed, crossing in the other direction. The faeries were quite literally changing over who had domain in this realm and who was in charge of the other. From spring to autumn, the apparent world is governed by the seelie court, and from autumn to spring is governed by the unseelie.

To be clear, this does not mean that every faery of the seelie type disappears for half the year, and visa versa. Think more of it like an ambassadorial convoy sent on a diplomatic mission with the different sides taking turns. Therefore, you are likely to see seelie Fae more in the summer months and unseelie in the winter, but we will talk about seasonal work in more detail later.

Anyway, back to the thorn gate. This vision of a tear between the worlds led to other work and seeking out other thorn gates. They aren't as easy to find as you might think, for they must satisfy the following conditions:

1. The two trees must be of the same species.
2. The two trees must be similarly sized and allowed to grow untrimmed.
3. It cannot be two trees overgrown in a hedge with other scrub between; there must be a clear passage that you can walk through.

Blackthorn and hawthorn are the two prime candidates for these gate configurations given their long connection with the faery realms. However, apple, oak, and rowan have also worked to an extent. Rowan is probably the easiest to find in the correct configuration within an urban area. However, the trees are often sickly, having been embedded in concrete or tarmac. Some also have metal cages around them to stop damage from dogs, cats, squirrels, and bored kids. This pretty much negates any possible faery energy, so results can be patchy, and don't forget that giving offerings to the scabby rowans at the end of the street at midnight might raise an eyebrow or two with the neighbors, so it's all going to be about your own personal comfort levels.

· EXERCISE ·
monitoring the thorn gate

Once you have identified a likely pair of trees and dowsed the area to see if you can pick anything up, the next stage toward making a connection is very simple. Make some offerings. My very first offering is nearly always one of time, for when working in urban environments, the chances are you are going to have to care for the site a bit before it will open up to you. Go with some gloves, a rubbish bag, and a litter picker and clear the area. If you can get away with it, talk to the trees and explain to them why you are clearing the space. Use your little voice if you have to. While few people will think much of someone doing a little bit of environmental cleanup in a neglected city or town park or green space, combine it with loud muttering and they might put you in the bag lady category and get the authorities to move you on. Next, consider appropriate offerings. If you live in an area where water shortages are common and hosepipe bans remain permanently in place during summer and winter, then a bottle of water poured at the roots of each tree will certainly go a long way toward warming up the relationship between the trees and their guardians.

One of the nice things about modern technology is that our practices don't always have to be about sitting at the foot of a tree in the dark night after night. A well-taken photograph will allow us to access the site remotely, regardless of weather, lunar phase, and if the location is a place you feel comfortable visiting alone. Talented artists can sketch, but a quick snap on a camera or phone is more than adequate and far more in keeping with our urban ethos and lifestyle. So, once you are happy a connection is made, try taking a photograph of the site and using it to scry for activity.

PORTAL IMAGE

Graffiti is a good example of using a portal image to access the otherworlds. I am completely and utterly obsessed with graffiti and the magick that inspires artists, but it doesn't have to be just graffiti; any artwork will do, be it Fae-inspired fantasy art, tarot cards, elemental symbols, and so on. You will know a Fae-inspired piece of art when you see it. There is a depth and energy about it that is different from other works of art.

Once you have found your image, you will need to work with it intensively to get the best results. Here are a few daily exercises you might like to try to build your confidence.

· EXERCISE ·
images

Print your chosen picture or make it the splash screen on your phone, tablet, or computer. Carry it with you or stick it to your bathroom mirror or on the tiles by the cooker. Basically, make sure you are noticing it both consciously and unconsciously all throughout your day. Do this for at least a week and keep a daily diary of unusual things that you see, things you have never noticed before, coincidences that seem related to the work you are doing, and, most of all, your dreams.

Now, I am a very vivid dreamer, but my daydreams are even stronger. I find that my daydreams have as much to tell me as my nocturnal ones do. In fact, whole sections of this book were inspired by my daydreams. The point is to write everything down, even if it doesn't make sense. Honestly, it doesn't have to. The Fae often don't. Much of this is about feeling—that stone in the bottom of your gut, the hairs tingling on the back of your neck, that slightly giddy, not-quite-with-it sensation. These can all be indicators of the other being close.

For further experimentation, take the image you have been working with and look at it. Make up a story about it and let your mind wander. In some ways, this exercise is the exact opposite of that much-valued technique of mindfulness. Here, we are practicing focused and conscious daydreaming. Let everything and anything pop into your brain and follow it wherever it takes you. The only rule to this exercise is to note when an image or thought has an extra depth or increased sensation. Write these things down after your wandering has finished. Eventually, you will be all imagined out; trust me. At which point, you need to write down key thoughts and ideas. Also, take unusual images and try to write a story about them. If possible, see if you can find a faery to play the starring role. You can bet that if your subconscious can dredge up a faery, there was one there in your little mental trip into the other, and from there, you can build a relationship.

Another interesting exercise to add to this task is the art of Google. On more than one occasion, I have heard a word or seen an image in my mind, and I have gone to Google looking for an answer. The word may be nonsense, but almost always I find something that inspires me as part of the process. While these portal image mental wanderings can be practiced very effectively alone, they are best used as the precursor to scrying the image in full.

TECHNIQUES FOR EFFECTIVE SCRYING

Scrying is a technique that is invaluable when dealing with the realms of Faerie because it is easier to communicate with the otherworlds through this practice than actually crossing over or using trance and journeying. History may be full of stories of humans entering a faery ring or fort and living to tell the tale (albeit often many years later), but the reality of it is that this is the exception, not the rule. If you haven't come across scrying before, consider it a bit like making a Skype call for a chat rather than hopping in a car for a visit. It is quicker, more convenient, and more accessible to everyone, for it is a skill that is easily learned and can be performed with minimum fuss.

Scrying has been written about by dozens of authors from almost as many different paths. A wealth of information is available on the subject, and yet there is often a lot of misunderstanding about this skill. Many people overcomplicate the practice with empty ritual and superstition. We all naturally scry when we daydream, although we may not realize that is what we are doing. Remember those warm summer days when you imagined the clouds in the sky were dragons and warriors, rabbits and motorcars, and your eyes slowly defocused, allowing you to drift into a heady world of imagination? What you were doing was free-form scrying, which is basically a more focused form of the imagination and portal image exercises we practiced earlier. Therefore, even if you've never attempted this practice before, if you've been following along with the exercises, it should really only require a brief look at the basics to get you up and running.

Thanks to the laws of sympathetic magick, choosing the medium in which to scry can amplify your efforts. Like will always call to like. Therefore, should you wish to work with a water sprite, it is advisable to collect some of the water from the river, reservoir, lake, or water butt in which you believe the sprite lives. Clear water isn't ideal, so placing it in a dark bowl or adding food coloring is a possibility, but any liquid medium can be used: treacle, red wine, and even coffee.

In popular culture, there is the concept of the absinthe faery, *la feé verte*, or the green faery, a thought-form that most definitely exists and, in my opinion, is a class 1 spirit. It's the spirit of wormwood that has been so transmuted by both the distilling process and the energy of group belief that it now has its own unique consciousness. Why not also have a red wine faery, a coffee pixie, or a beer brownie? Brownies and beer have been connected for a long time, and the creature known as the buttery sprite frequents bars and taverns all over the world, so see if you can find one the next time you visit a pub. Be creative and open-minded with the Fae whom you scry for and receive; they may come across as odd, but that doesn't mean that they aren't real.

Fire is another scrying medium; candle flames, open fires, and flammable gel in ceramic bowls are all great options if treated with due respect and caution, particularly when working indoors. But also consider other more urban light sources that you may come across. Sodium streetlights are essentially fire of metal, and neon and argon signage is fire of air, as it contains inert gases. All are well worth exploring as a potential medium for accessing the world of Faerie.

Highly polished wood on tabletops, doors, floorboards, and even chopping boards allows the mind to access the element of wood. And with wood, you have the interesting phenomenon of pareidolia (faces in objects), which, in my opinion, despite what the scientists say, is often a spirit shining through, not a mundane feature of the humane psyche, as some would have you believe. The same goes for metal; well-polished brass or steel plates, which can be bought from discount home furnishing stores, are a great tool. Even ceramic plates with a metallic glaze can work. They also look wonderfully inconspicuous sitting in plain view with a few scented pine cones or a handful of potpourris sitting on top.

Air is not so simple because you cannot physically see air itself. Apart from the neon and argon signs mentioned above, your options can be quite limited. The heat haze from your candle rather than the flame itself is air of fire. The smoke from your incense is heavily laden with particulates, so it is air of earth. Even clouds are essentially water suspended in the medium of air. Luckily, I've found that it is rarely necessary to scry air as a pure element. However, when I have tried, it is best to sit outside on a windy day or in front of a desk fan with your eyes closed, just sensing the air without any visuals.

You can get very creative with the elemental combinations. Pewter and lead-based metals can be heated into a liquid form to create water of metal, for example. Clay and water mixed into a thin slurry make water of earth. The red-hot lump of wood charcoal normally used in barbecues is fire of wood.

You can make the act of scrying a ritual performed within sacred spaces, or you can just get your things together and get the job done. It's going to all come down to your personal preferences and your location. However, as a species, we are highly ritualized and derive great meaning and comfort from creating patterns and connections, so I personally enjoy a little pomp and ceremony when I practice my craft. Sessions performed in low light add a depth to the atmosphere, allowing you to blank out the outside world; candlelight is ideal. If you are using a liquid medium, you will normally get better results if your light sources are positioned some distance away and at a lower level than the scrying device. This stops light reflections from bouncing off the surface, which can be very distracting.

· EXERCISE ·
how to scry the faery realms

Scrying for extended periods of time can lead to some considerable discomfort, which is why many people, myself included, suggest starting in a straight-backed chair with feet flat on the floor. However, this is not really practical when working in external urban locations where you may not be able to take a chair along with you. You may even have to stand because the location may be damp and dirty—and not in a "good clean dirt" kind of way. Although a lot of general grime can be mitigated by carrying a sturdy plastic bag in your pocket to sit on in a less-than-sanitary location, please be really cautious about where you sit; I don't want anybody getting ill.

However you choose to position yourself, the ideal is to have a straight back and to not be so comfortable that you are likely to doze off. I encourage you to experiment with a number of different positions to see which one is right for you. If you can manage it, sitting cross-legged can be very comfortable, but be aware that it may over time cause pins and needles in your ankles and feet, which can be extremely painful. A small meditation cushion or inflatable pillow, which can be stowed in a bag, is an excellent way of seating yourself cross-legged and relieving the pressure from the weight of your knees onto your lower extremities.

If you are working with mediums on location, such as puddles, human-made items filled with water, windows, brickwork, and so on, then the item to be scryed should be no more than fifty to seventy centimeters (twenty to thirty inches) away from your eyes; if this is at home, then it is actually preferable to go a little closer, say thirty to fifty centimeters (ten to twenty inches), for best effect. Items can be placed on a table in front of you, held in your hands, or set on a low altar if you are sitting on the floor. There are exceptions to this, such as graffiti, but this advice holds for the most part.

How you look into the medium also varies a little depending on the substance and the location. For fluids, it's advisable to avoid focusing your vision on the surface; instead, stare through the surface as if it were a window, imagining a focal point a short distance behind, say ten centimeters.

It's not advised to stare for long periods of time directly at a flame. You could damage your retina, and it will certainly have you seeing spots in front of your eyes for a long time afterward. Try focusing your vision just above the flame. If the environment is still and calm, it is possible to see that there is an aura or void area that surrounds the flame. This is where you want to aim. When using an open fire, to avoid eyestrain and dry eyes, I have found the ideal is to stare into the embers or the source of the flame rather than watching the flames themselves. Flame elementals do exist and are an interesting species, if not often very communicative, so try to see what you get.

By far the biggest tip for scrying is the following: *don't forget to blink!* We blink constantly in the mundane world, and we bodily remain in the mundane world when we scry, so why should blinking affect your visions of the otherworld? Truth is, your eyes are redundant when it comes to this practice, as it isn't really your eyes that are seeing when you scry; nothing at this point is passing into this realm, so this generally holds true for extreme sensitives as well. However, failure to blink will cause discomfort, and that is a surefire way of bringing your session to a swift end. Which would be a big shame if you were making some kind of first contact.

STATE YOUR INTENT

Your childhood daydreams were essentially random, unfocused scrying: delightfully entertaining, but often not a lot more. Having no focus or control over the activity can even be counterproductive. It can also result in interference from undesirables. Therefore, having a specific purpose in mind and stating it clearly goes a long way to ensure that what you are tapping into is what you are expecting. So, start with your general statement of intent. For example,

I call to the universe to witness this rite, to aid me in contacting the realms of the creatures of Fae, that they may tell me what I need to know.

Once comfortable, you may want to use one of the following charms before you start your work. They are adaptations of old English folk charms, so they have some providence. They are best chanted in a multiple of three, and once you have built a rapport with a particular entity, you can substitute in its name, calling it directly rather than just calling out blindly, hoping someone will answer (although, if your dowsing has been effective, it shouldn't be a blind hope). Once you feel comfortable enough, you should try writing your own summoning charm that can be tailored to the Fae you are working with. For the time being, you could choose to use an adaptation of existing charms.

> *Come in the stillness, come in the night, come soon,*
> *and bring delight. Beckoning, beckoning, left hand and right,*
> *spirit of* [insert element here], *reveal yourself tonight!*
> *Faery fair and faery bright, come and be my chosen sprite,*
> *spirit of* [element], *appear to my sight!*

MORE ON GRAFFITI
AND ITS USES IN SCRYING

It is possible to scry in just about anything: water, oil, tarot cards, and so on. And my personal favorite is graffiti. I have maintained for a long time that, where once we might have sought out the Fae in unusual formations of rocks, plants, or trees and even in the water pools and swirls on a riverbank, now we feel the traces of the urban Fae in the artwork scrawled in underpasses and dark alleys. They lurk just on the edge of our vision and inspire those of us who are sensitive and, for time immemorial, the artists and revolutionaries among us who have been known for their visionary abilities.

There is a particular loathly lady who is the faery equivalent of a wild child: mystifying, intoxicating, and inspiring. The leannan sídhe, whose name quite literally means "faery lover," is said to be the muse of many an artist or poet. None of her tales are particularly wholesome. She keeps her lovers trapped in her thrall until they either find another person to love or are driven mad by her tender ministrations. An exquisite death: slowly being drained of life, sucked dry while all the time creating the most breathtaking works of art, music, or writing.

Things have not changed much, in my opinion. If you see a particularly inspiring piece of artwork, the likelihood is that there is a touch of the other about it. The magickal artist Austin Osman Spare created some outstanding and powerful images and sigils during his time on earth, and no person I know who has witnessed these images firsthand has ever failed to be moved by the power contained within them. However, their copies (particularly electronic ones), while still energetic, aren't quite so overwhelming, as if the process of reproduction has diluted the potency. The same is true of graffiti images. At the end of each chapter focusing on the elements, I will include scrying artwork that has inspired and prompted me to think of that element. The images have been very specifically chosen because they are relatively safe and perfect for learning this technique.

Work with the images provided and get used to them before you go seeking out any of your own. Quite simply, don't run before you can walk, and start your experiments in a controlled environment. I've spent many a happy hour tracking down what I believe to be Fae-inspired artwork, but very few of the images I have connected most with have been situated in positions that make it easy to spend hours experimenting with the image and using it as any form of astral portal. As with the thorn gate and faery ring exercises, photographs are just fine, so use them.

Unlike elemental scrying, you may consider the image to be a door or a portal that you can either choose to walk through or ask a faery spirit to come forth from. In early experiments, I would suggest the latter. The rest is pretty much the same technique as previously described. Sit comfortably, breathe normally, perhaps defocus your eyes a little, and don't forget to blink.

the elements

Fairies Black, Grey, Green and White
You moonshine revellers and shades of night
You Orphan heirs of fixed destiny
Attend your office and your quality.[28]

Most people are aware of the classical elemental system of earth, air, fire, and water. First suggested as a system by Empedocles somewhere around the mid-fifth century BCE, each element has been developed and expanded and has been assigned colors, angels, cardinal directions, planets, four separate species of spirit, and even mottos. Some traditions call these races of spirits "elementals," and, to some extent, this description fits. The renowned alchemist and occultist Paracelsus named them gnomes, sylphs, salamanders, and undines. Many who have undergone any in-depth study or training will recognize these names along with the names of their kings, as they have almost become synonymous with the Fae.

The problem is, not all faeries fit neatly into these boxes. This was a conundrum I contemplated on and off for a considerable length of time, and after struggling with the nature of one particular entity, it occurred to me that this form of classification alone might not be the solution. After all, the Fae exist all over the world. I started to look afield. While questioning the entity about my suspicions, I was led to the conclusion that the world of the Fae is more easily described by using a combination of the classical Western four-element system and the Taoist five-element system. Of course, this still isn't completely

---

28. William Shakespeare, *The Merry Wives of Windsor* (Hertfordshire, UK: Wordsworth Editions, 1996), 579.

foolproof, but I am reliably informed that it is as close an approximation as our limited minds will be able to understand.

A BRIEF LAYMAN'S HISTORY OF THE WU XING

The Chinese system of element classification, or wu xing, is significantly older than the Western. I beg patience of those who work in depth with this system; the following explanation is deliberately brief, as wu xing is a complex and highly evolved system taking years of study to master, and I heartily recommend further exploration if this brief introduction grabs you. The main purpose for now is to understand how the two kinds of elements can be combined when working with the Fae.

According to Littlejohn, the earliest recognizable evidence of the Chinese system of elements was somewhere between 1600 and 1046 BCE.[29] The system was carved on bones, which were used as a form of oracle. It was a simplistic five-point system that had a rudimentary set of correspondences associated with it. These correspondences included colors, cardinal directions, and deities. Does this sound familiar? This was widely adopted and developed further, so by the time of the Han dynasty in the third century, it more closely resembled the system that is known today.

One reference from that period is of particular interest to us. In the twenty-seventh year of Duke Xiang, it was revealed that heaven created five elements.[30] These elements were created to provide for humanity, and not one element could be omitted.

These basic materials were associated with tastes, colors, sounds, and even magickal guardians who were responsible for the well-being and care of the elements. These magickal beings were known as the officers of the elements. This is similar to our four elemental kings: Ghob, Nicksa, Paralda, and Djinn.

---

29. R. Littlejohn, "Wuxing (Wu-hsing)," Internet Encyclopedia of Philosophy, accessed October 31, 2019, https://iep.utm.edu/wuxing/.

30. University of Virginia, "The Chunqiu; with the Zuo Zhuan," Traditions of Exemplary Women, accessed October 31, 2019, http://www2.iath.virginia.edu/saxon/servlet/Saxon Servlet?source=xwomen/texts/chunqiu.xml&style=xwomen/xsl/dynaxml.xsl&chunk .id=d2.16&toc.depth=1&toc.id=0&doc.lang=bilingual.

It was said that these officers "were sacrificed [after death] as Spirits, and received honour and offerings. The chief officer of wood was called Goumang; of fire, Zhurong; of metal, Rushou; of water, Xuanming; of earth, Houtu."[31]

The officers were also responsible for the care of magickal creatures associated with each element. Failure by these officers to perform their duties would result in the creature failing to appear or reproduce. One such failure is the reason that dragons no longer exist.

HOW DO DRAGONS RELATE TO OUR MODERN WORLD?

So what, I hear you ask, do Chinese dragons have to do with Cornish piskies or Scots kelpies? Quite simply, they are also creatures of the Fae. And if the Chinese myths are to be believed, dragons can cease to appear—maybe even exist—because of a lack of care, understanding, and interaction. If other creatures are to avoid this fate, then it is our obligation to learn how to become the officers of the elemental creatures, the guardians of their stories and sacred places. To do that, we must at the very least make an attempt to understand who they are, what they do, how best to relate to them, and how they now survive and exist in this thoroughly modern world.

SO HOW DOES IT WORK?

Others may have previously combined the elements in the same manner as shown below. As far as I am aware, it is not usual to assign these elemental attributions with the inhabitants of the otherworld. With this system, Fae of the same species whose attributes do not fit exclusively within one specific category or another can be more adequately described. Clear as mud? Well, hopefully the following explanation will help. The Western elemental system understands that each discrete element is actually four composite parts containing the other elements as follows:

- Air of air, fire of air, water of air, earth of air
- Fire of fire, water of fire, earth of fire, air of fire
- Water of water, earth of water, air of water, fire of water
- Earth of earth, air of earth, fire of earth, water of earth

31. Ibid.

Note: I have often debated if the element of spirit should also be included in this theory. But my experiences with the other has never led me to meet a spirit faery. Therefore, it has always felt a little redundant, particularly as, in my worldview, we are all creatures of spirit. The manner in which my system combines the Eastern and Western systems follows a very similar process, with each of the Eastern elements combining to make aspects of the Western (or vice versa), as can be seen in the table below.

	Wood	Fire	Metal	Water	Earth
Earth	Earth of Wood	Earth of Fire	Earth of Metal	Earth of Water	Earth of Earth
Air	Air of Wood	Air of Fire	Air of Metal	Air of Water	Air of Earth
Fire	Fire of Wood	Fire of Fire	Fire of Metal	Fire of Water	Fire of Earth
Water	Water of Wood	Water of Fire	Water of Metal	Water of Water	Water of Earth

Therefore, a being who is traditionally considered a water elemental may well actually be earth of water. Or, as with one of the entities I have worked with, fire of water. Another being may be air of metal rather than entirely air. Yet another, earth of wood, and so on.

In the following chapters, we will look at each of the elements in turn, studying them and some associated Fae in more detail. Through practical work and meditation, we can start to understand the good folk who are now inhabiting our town squares and city streets. For each element, we will follow a case study for a particular Fae, getting to know them within environments where you may not have thought to find them. We will also look at techniques you can develop to build your own relationships with the spirits in our increasingly broken land.

CHAPTER 8
WOOD

I went out to the hazel wood,
Because a fire was in my head,
And cut and peeled a hazel wand,
And hooked a berry to a thread.[32]

The ability to align and balance yourself with each of the elements will help you not only to gain a better balance in your life, but also to gain a greater understanding of the spirits in the world around you. Knowing the essence of a thing is almost as important as knowing the name of a thing, for once you know its inherent nature, it is easy to anticipate how it will react and interact. In the following chapters, we shall look in turn at each of the five Eastern elements, work with them, and study various urban Fae that fall under each element. I will also provide references to various other common urban Fae that fall under these categories for you to investigate further, both theoretically through researching their myths as well as physically through seeking them out.

I have started with wood because it is listed first in the wu xing. Each of the five elements or essences are associated with a season, but hanging around waiting for the start of a cycle, which is essentially a human construct, seems like a waste of time. Therefore, you may like to start according to the season you are currently experiencing. I suggest you read the remainder of the book thoroughly once and then return to the correct exercises for that period of time.

32. W. B. Yeats, *Fairy and Folk Tales of the Irish Peasantry* (London: Walter Scott, 1888).

MODERN SIGHTINGS—
THE ZARAGOZA GOBLIN

In 1934 in the city of Zaragoza, Spain, the Palazón family was plagued by a very unusual and decidedly unwelcome guest in their apartment block.[33] It started with banging, laughter, and screaming that seemed to be coming from the walls and the chimney. The situation turned even more sinister when the perpetrator started targeting a young maid named Pascuala Alocer, calling out her name and mocking her, scaring the poor girl half to death.

Believing it to be a rowdy neighbor, the Palazón family started by involving the police. The entire building was searched for the troublemaker, but with no success. Even more curious was that the voice started holding conversations with the people who didn't run away. The police actually questioned the voice, asking it what it wanted and why it was causing trouble. Did he want money, food, a job? The response was always just "no" until finally the frustrated police officer demanded, "Then what is it you want, man?" The voice replied, "Nothing, I am not a man."[34]

The exchanges continued all through the autumn and into the winter of 1934, and various experts were called in to investigate the phenomena, including a priest, who is said to have blessed the entire building, but apparently to no avail, as the insults and disruption continued. Some people tried to blame the young maid, claiming that the voice was the result of her practicing "unconscious ventriloquism," even though some of the incidents occurred when the poor girl was not in the building. As a result of these accusations, she was eventually fired and returned to her village, but not before the voice, now being called a duende (the Spanish name for a specific sort of goblin), had issued his final ominous warning, crying, "Cowards, cowards, here I am, I will kill everyone in the room," resulting in the Palazón family fleeing their apartment forever.[35]

---

33. E. Grundhauser, "Unconscious Ventriloquism: The Unsolved Mystery of the Zaragoza Goblin," Atlas Obscura, accessed September 30, 2019, https://www.atlasobscura.com/articles/unconscious-ventriloquism-the-unsolved-mystery-of-the-zaragoza-goblin.

34. History Disclosure Team, "Duende de Zaragoza: The Case of a Talking Entity," History Disclosure, accessed October 30, 2019, https://www.historydisclosure.com/duende-de-zaragoza-case-talking-entity/.

35. Ibid.

Although many over the years have tried to claim that the entire incident was an elaborate hoax, there has never been any solid evidence to prove that was the case. When comparing the story to other existing folklore, it's very obviously a case of a disgruntled house spirit, one which, until that point, had been happily living in an apartment block in the middle of a busy city.

Most domestic spirits such as brownies, boggarts, pixies, duendes, nisse, and tomte should be considered wood elemental spirits. In the wu xing, the element of wood is associated with spring and the planet Jupiter. It is an element of expansion, development, and activity. And while wood is associated with various aspects we would normally attribute to Jupiter, such as success in endeavors related to wealth, finance, and material assets, it also relates to some aspects of life that would normally be associated with other elements: family and relations, the more cerebral creative projects (research and writing), the arts, and culture all fall into the realm of wood. Our domestic helper spirits, as a rule, concern themselves with all these matters.

Wood doesn't just relate to trees, either. It includes a wide range of organic matter, so plant divas of all types will often fall under this category as well. And in addition to the domestic spirits, certain other household spirits may also fit here, particularly any that have anything to do with books and places of study or artistic activities. For example, I have a "book toad" who resides in my study. The more disorganized and overflowing my shelves are, the happier this little creature is. I use him regularly to help me retain information and to find passages and phrases in books when researching. He is definitely air of wood, for although he sits firmly in the realm of wood, his activities are highly cerebral and, therefore, also of the element of air.

CASE STUDY 1:
THE SPIRIT OF THE APPLE BARREL

My first personal case study is, or should I say was, a dryad, although he has not been recognizably so in at least one hundred years. I found this little fella in the cellars of a guest house in Shropshire. The guest house was rather large and decadent. It had been rented out by a group of my friends and colleagues so that we could share knowledge, experience, and ritual together.

Anybody who works with magick tends to be rather nosy; it's part of what makes us who we are. So, true to form, we all set about investigating the property and its surrounding land upon arrival. Several people claimed that there was something lurking in the dark and damp cellar, but nobody stayed long enough to discover its source, as they were overwhelmed by the smell of mold and rancid cider apples and a healthy desire to keep clear of things that go bump in the dark. Not sure what the fact that I persevered says about me, but there you go.

Initially, the creature refused to make himself visible but called out from the dark, naming himself as Bar-El. He remembered that he had once been a free spirit in the woods, the dryad of a great oak tree, and he knew he was now something different, something more of this world. He also shared his fear of death a number of times, claiming he was rotting and one day he would no longer have a home. A sense of mortality is actually a commonality both the first and second species of urban Fae seem to share; mortality is not normally known to creatures of the other.

This sense of mortality intrigued me. Why would this faery think it was rotting and destined to die? I had to find out why. At the back of the cellar among assorted rusting agricultural tools was a large apple barrel, and upon its discovery, a little face appeared in the knots of the wood. Finally, all became clear—Bar-El was a barrel! A barrel dark and discolored at its base, showing signs of mildew and water damage no doubt from its less-than-dry location.

Once the little guy worked out that I wasn't there to chop him up for firewood, something I suspect he may have been threatened with before, he would creep out and come to the foot of the stairs of the cellar, allowing for a far more comfortable way of interacting. He was a wistful character with fragmented memories of green leaves and laughter, a time before his tree was chopped down and turned into the barrel in which he now lived. I liken the trauma this caused him to that which is suffered as the result of a major accident or stroke. The trauma was so great that his memories became incomplete, a form of selective amnesia that is nature's way of easing the pain.

He was also very protective of the house, the cellar, and the barrel in which he lived. He felt his purpose now was as a guardian spirit for these objects and the place. He had quite literally evolved into the genius loci. So when I offered the option to relocate, he initially showed no desire to leave, believing it was his fate to accept mortality and eventually fade as the barrel disintegrated into pulp.

The thought that there may be an alternative was not something that had crossed his mind. After spending the week, I made a suggestion. I took some grass from the property and braided a crude form of fetish, a connection to the energy of that place, and I promised to buy him a small barrel as a place he could call a sanctuary should living in his current home become untenable. I would place the fetish with the barrel so that he could find it. I promised that should he arrive one day in that barrel, I would go out of my way to find him something more permanent in which he could live out the remainder of his days.

That was in 2008, and apart from the odd times he has popped in to check up on me, he has not taken me up on my offer. He may never do so, choosing instead to fade away or even to relocate somewhere else in the house, for he is not tied completely to the barrel. He may come to the conclusion himself that he can choose his own home, but this has left me with an interesting conundrum. Fae do not experience time in the same way we do. I might not even be alive when he arrives in his temporary accommodation. I might have created a family legacy that will require guardianship across generations. I might even have created the situation where a spirit is attached to a family. This is actually not uncommon, and we shall look at a few more examples of this later in the chapter. It is a huge responsibility, and I will say my realization of this rash commitment has made me a little less eager to help spirits in need of relocation.

There are ways around this little issue, one that may explain many strange and usual things found in gaps in chimneys, cemented into cavities in walls, and lodged into dry cracks in caves, and that is to find a safe place for Bar-El to remain, unharmed and untouched by human hands. It feels somewhat a lonely existence, but that is probably just a human construct. Should you ever choose to follow a rescue and relocate policy, this may be the best solution. Don't make a promise your descendants cannot keep!

ALIGNING YOURSELF WITH WOOD

Understanding the nature of wood isn't all about sitting under a tree for hours or hugging it until you feel its heartbeat (although these are very rewarding activities and even scientists are saying they're good for your health). This is a book about urban Fae after all, and at times our connection with nature and the wild isn't an easy one, so these exercises reflect that.

While you are working with these elements, you may want to bring aspects of them into your daily life to help with the process of aligning. You could try scrying the knots in wooden items, eating only wood-related foods (basically, a plant-based diet), looking for shapes in tree bark and patterns in leaves, and wearing only wood colors. And I know I said it wasn't about tree hugging, but please try to go hug a tree!

· EXERCISE ·
finding the spirit of wood

The first part of this exercise is to find something made of wood that has been manufactured or shaped by human hands. It needs to either be small enough to hold in your hands or in a position that you can sit comfortably on it, against it, or with your hands touching it for a reasonable period of time. These items can be everyday and do not have to have any deep occult significance. Possible items may be the following:

- An old park bench or a dining chair
- A wooden trinket box
- An antique fan
- A pencil

I strongly suggest that you stay away from medium-density fiberboard, ply, and particle board, at least until you've got a good sense of what you are doing. So, mass-market flatpack furniture isn't going to be a great choice. In my experience, any essence that may remain in these items is so fragmented that it's just not a worthwhile exercise.

When attempting this exercise, pick a time when you aren't going to be disturbed for a while and start by spending a few minutes working with the verdant breath. Allow the spirit of ivy to cleanse your body and mind, preparing you for the work ahead.

Start by holding the item and sensing it. I find that having your eyes open can often restrict our sensations because we overlay everything with a visual, but you may have your eyes open or closed; it is up to you. The point is to take your time to really feel the object.

Is the item smooth or rough? Can you feel any energy from it? Does that energy feel human-made or made by something else? Is it dormant or is it responding to your touch? How does it make you feel—happy, sad, uncomfortable, safe? Take as long as you need to explore the item, and then write about the experience. You will find that certain objects may have a very human-made energy about them and yet still feel very alive. These are often objects that have a long history or some kind of sentimental value. What you are feeling is really more a constructed thought-form than a wood spirit. That's okay. It's still worth exploring so that you can tell the difference between the two.

Please don't rule out new objects thinking they will have nothing about them. Quite the opposite. It is precisely because they are new that the spirits' original essence will not have degraded so much, making any energy quite raw and vibrant. Just as some people believe that young children have a much greater capacity to remember past lives, it does seem that newly processed and manufactured items often retain a muscle memory of their past existence for some time. Bar-El was quite an unusual example in that; although his tree had been gone for over one hundred years, his memories were still intact enough to make out his original form. This will not always be the case in an older object, so new can actually be far more rewarding from a research and feedback perspective.

The second part of the exercise is to take this one step further and imagine yourself as the piece of wood. How do you feel to its touch? What energy is it sensing from you? How do you make it feel? If you were it, would you want to make contact? Why? Trust your instincts and your imagination. Remember, imagination is a skill that has served humanity well. The more you use it, the better your connection will become.

....

CASE STUDY 2: CARRICK, THE GUARDIAN OF THE THORN GATE

In the spring of 2009, I decided to explore the idea of the faery portal, a concept that I had become aware of the previous year. As we discussed in chapter 6, the premise of a faery portal created by a thorn gate is very simple. Certain pairings of trees where a path or thoroughfare passes through are hot spots for faery manifestation. The first pairing I found purely by chance were two apple trees at the entrance to an ancient orchard that had been carved up to make way for a bypass road circumnavigating a busy northern town. It had struck me that urban planting and the remnants of old hedgerows often left in situ in new developments might lend themselves to these portals being easy to find in urban environments, and so it is.

Further experimentation yielded a pairing of oak trees near my current home and two friendly dryads who introduced themselves to me through meditation and journeying. Initially, I suspected they were just the elemental spirits of the trees themselves, but further work revealed that they were guardians of these portals. These were examples of class 2 spirits. They were aware to some extent of their previous existence in a more natural environment, but they had changed significantly as a result of the human interference in the form of the tarmac pathway that now separated these two siblings. Their own desire to adapt had sadly also wrought its own changes.

Thus ensued a delightful summer sitting under trees. Although, I did get a lot of odd looks from various neighbors and passersby! My biggest discoveries were that the trees had to be of the same genus for the portal to manifest and that the portal needed to be guarded by a pair of guardian Fae, some of which were more sentient than others. The sentience did have some bearing on the strength of the portal. However, this need for two trees of the same species to achieve an optimal gateway or portal is not surprising considering the findings that are now coming out in the field of dendrology.

Trees have interlinked roots reaching deep into the earth, far deeper sometimes than our asphalt roads and concrete foundations can reach. Trees have family units and the ability to warn trees in far-flung corners of the wood or forest that danger is imminent. Trees that stand side by side are often siblings having sprouted from acorns dropped from the same parent tree. It isn't too much of a stretch to realize that, genetically and energetically, if one of these particular arboreal offspring is suitable for Fae inhabitation, the other would be also. Therefore, it makes sense that the most active and potent portals are the result of close familial bonds between the guardians.

However, the most sentient and active gate I have ever come across has an unusual setup and breaks all the rules: a pairing of blackthorn and hawthorn. Despite the commonality in names, these two trees are from entirely different genera. This portal had only one sentinel: a rather dapper gentleman with bright purple eyes and no sclera (a very common physical feature in many inhabitants of the other-realms). He was the indwelling Fae in the blackthorn tree, his sloelike eyes being the giveaway. Blackthorn has a very long history of magick and faery association. A stout blackthorn staff or wand, often called a blasting rod, is believed to banish pretty much any spirit, the good folk or otherwise. It is now often planted by councils in the UK to repopulate hedge-rows, as its long needlelike thorns make great barriers and it is relatively swift-growing, with an early blossom and late fruit (although it rarely fruits before its tenth year) that encourages and protects the wildlife that is returning to urban and industrialized areas. Given time to grow and develop, though, these bushes become quite amazing twisted and gnarled trees, increasing the number of faery portals in urban environments.

When I first came across Carrick, he was an angry Fae indeed. This anger was thanks to the remnants of his very ancient hedge, which was situated at the edge of a newly developed housing estate and had been severed in two by a joyrider who had crashed a stolen car through it and left the car to rot in a ditch nearby. When I discovered the car, it was very rusty, almost unidentifiable. The gap left in the hedge never closed, as over time local residents made a pathway through to the undeveloped land beyond—now an unofficial community space for children to play and adults to walk the dog.

Upon my discovery of Carrick, he did everything to discourage me from investigating him: nausea, headache, fear, and dread as if the end of the world were upon me, and finally, an almost full corporeal manifestation of a shadow person hunched and menacing on top of the wrecked car. It was impressive. It took a lot of milk and honey and eventually an offering of sloes brought from The Howk, a faery location I will discuss in chapter 11, to appease him enough to interact with me. The relationship was mostly an uneasy one, which I would class as a respectful nodding of heads when I happened to be in the area. It wasn't until I moved to a new house that I fully realized the potential and the power of the blackthorn.

Not long after I moved from the outskirts of Manchester to the slightly more suburban Merseyside, I was woken night after night with night sweats, existential dread, and images of Carrick in my mind. Bright purple eyes loomed above my face. Several times, I was woken, believing there to be a shadow person in the house, but no amount of dowsing, meditation, or journeying could reveal the reason for my trouble. I was at a loss. It was only on the fourth day that I became aware that our local council was in the area, aggressively trimming all the trees on the roads and in the green spaces between the houses, pretty much butchering everything in sight. On that fourth morning, they were about to start on the young blackthorn hedge that was right in front of my house. I wasn't as successful in saving the young blackthorns as I would have liked—they still got far more of a haircut than was necessary—but I did stop the workers from pouring gallons of a particular brand of weed killer all around their roots, so a small victory was had thanks to a psychic connection with a Fae some thirty-five miles away.

Carrick has been one of my biggest learning experiences so far in that his existence, wants, desires, and level of sentience is far different from other wood-type Fae I have encountered. First, blackthorn guardians have the ability to create their own faery gates, something that none of the other species appear able to do. The most powerful of these gates happen when the pairing of trees is with another well-known faery tree species, such as hawthorn. Second, even the most traumatic of landscape changes and destruction wrought by man has little effect on their classification; they resolutely remain class 3 spirits. Finally, once a connection or affinity to their kin has been established, it is indelible.

Making connection to blackthorn Fae becomes second nature, and this is a very powerful and valuable tool, as they can be your protection and your guide when exploring a new area. If you can locate a blackthorn tree even without an indwelling spirit, then a previous connection to a blackthorn Fae means that you have an ally to call on if you sense trouble (and as with the case of Carrick, vice versa). This makes carrying a wand, staff, or blackthorn amulet made from a few twigs doubly useful. You are also on the homeward stretch to making a connection to the other Fae in that area, as you can call for any other blackthorn spirit known to you to act as an intermediary.

· MEDITATION ·
Journey to the Spirit of Wood

Allow your perception of the mundane world to slip quietly away, the image of reality dissolving and blowing away like the wind, mist swirling around you, gray, green, sickly yellow. It obscures your vision and numbs your senses. This mist hangs dense, forming condensation on your eyelids, in your hair. Plumes of thick breath billow out in front of you. You feel deeply rooted in this place between places. Take a few moments to ensure you have fully immersed yourself in this other space. This is neither here nor there, a staging point to allow you to acclimatize. Breathe normally. There is nothing to fear.

Slowly, the mist parts, dissipating almost as quickly as it arrived. But now you find yourself in a large room. It is four-sided, a square, and upon the floor are tiles of white marble and black onyx with a fabulous citrine dragon inlaid upon them. The north is directly in front of you, the south behind, east to your right, west to your left. Upon each wall is a brightly illustrated mural depicting various magickal beasts. Turning to the right and the east, you face the image of an emerald-green serpent. Its scales glint like jewels. You realize that this image is painted upon ancient wooden doors, heavily grained and studded in places worn shiny with use.

Your heart beats slowly in your chest, and you can feel the essence of joy and spring flowing through your veins, pumping life, growth, and harmony into you. The swoosh of blood in your ears is now layered with the rustle of the wind in the trees and with birdsong. A warm green light seeps under the door, flickering and dancing. Take a deep breath and push the door open.

You step through into a circular room, every inch of which is covered in shelving stacked precariously full of books. This is the world tree, the akashic record, the library of Alexandria. It is all those things and none. It holds the knowledge of both humans and Fae alike. The floor beneath you is rich green moss studded with tiny blue and white flowers—speedwell, a plant of healing and magick. On the far wall is a hearth. A small fire burns in the grate, and on either side of the fire are two large wing-backed chairs; between them is a table holding two glasses of a golden sparkling fluid. A hand reaches out from one of the chairs to take a glass and a face follows, peering around the wing of the armchair. A curly-haired youth with a coronet of daisies and forget-me-nots in his hair beckons you forward.

He hands you a book. It is leather-bound, buttery soft to touch, and upon it are five engraved symbols. Take note of these symbols; they are the seeds of your work with the Fae. The beginnings of ideas. You try to open the book, but there is a large clasp with a lock, and you have no key. The youth smiles and shakes his head. Although he speaks no words, you know that now is not the time to open the book. The symbols are message enough. Another time, maybe. You bow to the youth and take a single step back. The moss dissolves, and you find yourself on the tiled floor once again. Take a moment here and commit the symbols on the book to memory. Don't rush to return to reality just yet; this place is designed as a buffer to allow you to process what you have seen, a world between worlds.

When you are ready, call out and ask that the mist may come to carry you home, to the here and now.

....

FINDING OTHER FAE

Below are other Fae whom you may find readily in urban locations. Consider these when you come across any particular spirit who strikes you as a wood Fae.

THE APPLE TREE MAN

This is a Fae who exists in the oldest tree in the orchard. As an urban myth, he has benefited from a resurgence in popularity and gained a large following. This is probably due to his story being retold in popular culture. The series *Supernatural* instantly springs to mind, although he has been portrayed in other films and various websites (not necessarily in the most favorable light).

You would be forgiven for thinking that he is primarily a nature Fae rather than an urban one, but with towns expanding and large landowners selling to developers, remnants of old apple orchards can be found in gardens, on road-sides, and as part of municipal parkland in city centers. In the UK, we are also seeing whole new "orchards" growing along the borders of expressways and motorways thanks to people throwing their apple cores out windows as they drive by. As a result, the apple tree man's habitat is actually expanding in very urban ways.

Once identified, you can petition him for help in anything where you need a "bountiful harvest," so any kind of work, business, or prosperity matter. Remember, the Fae have an unusual concept of money, so be very specific. Like a lot of Fae, his powers can be somewhat seasonal, and although he can be contacted all year round, he is best petitioned the same way as his rural counterpart—with wassailing, normally between the fifth and the seventeenth of January.[36]

HAMADRYADS, MELIAE, AND OTHER WOOD SPIRITS

Trees thankfully haven't completely disappeared from our urban spaces. Even on the busiest city street, you will find plants and trees, even if they are only in pots and human-made beds. Although it may seem unlikely that you would encounter a Fae, you may be surprised. Some species have adapted particularly well to empty lots and restricted growing spaces, so don't discount them.

In Greek mythology, there are a large number of tree spirits. Hamadryads are a specific familial group inhabiting eight different species:

- Karya (walnut or hazelnut)
- Balanos (oak)
- Kraneia (dogwood)
- Morea (mulberry)
- Aigeiros (black poplar)
- Ptelea (elm)
- Ampelos (vines, especially Vitis)
- Syke (fig)

Sadly, in some regions, you will struggle to find some of these trees to work with. Mulberry, while once prolific across all of Europe, North Africa, and India, is now very hard to find in the UK. But never fear; just because we don't have extensive documentary evidence of faeries existing in a certain species of tree, doesn't mean that they don't. As we already know, ivy, hawthorn,

---

36. L. Cooper, *The Element Encyclopedia of Fairies: An A-Z of Fairies, Pixies, and Other Fantastical Creatures* (Falkirk, Scotland: Harper Element, 2014).

blackthorn, and the species above all have spirits. However, as with plant divas, while every individual plant may contain a spiritual essence, not every plant or tree will have a sentient indwelling spirit. If they did, then sightings would be far more common. Like with all the other elements, you will have to hunt down your inhabited tree.

Meliae, or the ash tree spirits, are particularly common in urban environments. The tree is tenacious, self-seeding in gutters of abandoned buildings, cracks in concrete, and basically anywhere it can get the tiniest root hold. The Meliae in Greek mythology were a pair of sisters who nursed the infant Zeus; they are incredibly protective guardians once a level of trust has been established. Suitable offerings to them are milk and honey.

Buddleia, sometimes known as the butterfly bush, is another species to look out for in the verges of abandoned lots and on the roofs of deserted buildings. It is found growing natively across Asia, Africa, and the Americas, and although not indigenous to Europe, it was introduced from the Caribbean in the 1700s. It is both prolific and tenacious and can often be seen in the same places where graffiti is found. As such, it is quite a good indicator of potential Fae activity, even if no actual spirit can be found indwelling.

· EXERCISE ·
Graffiti scrying image activity

You may like to use this image to practice elemental graffiti scrying (discussed in chapter 6).

Portal for the Element of Wood—Lanjarón, Spain
Photographed by Tara Sanchez

fire

The quivering nostril and the large eye,
That showed they were made of fire and flame,
Not dull and heavy Earth. [37]

Fire has the ability to both create and destroy; without fire, humanity would never have risen beyond much more than intelligent apes. Prometheus stole fire from the gods, giving it to humanity and thus allowing them to forge weapons. Like it or not, many of our biggest technological advances have happened during times of strife. It is the essence of early summer, a time of growth and expansion. In Eastern philosophies, the element of fire is thought to correspond to politics, innovation, and human development. Also, things that bizarrely flourish almost immediately after a period of conflict. And although we would normally associate many of these aspects with elemental air in Western traditions, considering humanity's intimate connection with fire and evolution, it is not too surprising that fire is associated with such worthy correspondences in other cultures.

MODERN SIGHTINGS— ENCOUNTERS WITH THE DJINN

Islamic lore states that the angels were created from light and the djinn were created from smokeless fire. Although not immortal, djinn have a vastly extended life span and existed before the creation of humanity. They possess superior intellect, strength, and build, making them formidable opponents if you happen to run into one who is in a bad mood. History also states that

---

37. B. Froud and A. Lee, *Faeries* (New York: Harry N. Abrams, 1978).

djinn were punished for eavesdropping on the angels and sent to live in a form of alternate world away from humanity, not dissimilar to the idea of the Irish Tuatha Dé Danann, who were tricked into living in a magickal otherworld beneath the earth after they lost their war against the Milesians. Curiously, some folktales also claim that djinn are deathly afraid of iron, which also parallels many European folk beliefs. Just like the Celtic Fae, djinn can and do visit our human realm—sometimes to help humans, more often to hinder, as they are considered the ultimate tricksters. Very occasionally, they are known to intermarry with a willing human. Some remote tribes claim family ties to specific djinn and are very proud of this lineage, claiming that they possess psychic and shamanistic abilities as a result.

While modern-day sightings of the djinn in the Arab world are almost daily with some towns almost famous for their infestations of these fire Fae, it is difficult to include these regular sightings as valid examples because, unlike with the Fae of Western cultures, djinn are still a real and tangible part of everyday life with many devout Muslims believing wholeheartedly in their existence. In my day job, I often come into contact with young Muslims, and upon learning that I am a Pagan, the first question they ask is, "Do you believe in djinn?" In situations like this, it is quite hard to separate fact from fiction. What is startling and worthy of note, though, is the sheer quantity of English and American service personnel who have reported supernatural activity in the Middle East, often on busy city streets, that can only be ascribed to the djinn of legend.

The retired soldier and member of the infamous Stargate program David Morehouse described one such encounter from his time in Jordan during the late 1980s during which he was woken from his sleep by a blinding light shining into his tent. Deciding to investigate, he found the entire town overrun by shadow beings who seemed to be set on torturing the local Jordanians. However, when he turned to confront one such creature, it ran straight through him as if it were made of smoke. His was not the only djinn encounter experienced by soldiers stationed across the Middle East in the last forty or so years. Others have reported inhuman beings with catlike eyes of flame being chauffeured through the streets of Mosul, animals shape-shifting into humanoid beings, and attacks by an incorporeal entity using crescent-shaped weapons of light like a supernatural version of throwing stars. The fire Fae are definitely alive and well, if we are willing to look for them.[38]

CASE STUDY 1:
THE LAR OF ANGER—
A DISPLACED BLUECAP

I'd been living in my last home a number of years before I decided to dowse to find and possibly awaken the house spirit. When my daughter was small, I'd made the decision to keep the inside of my house as "clean" as possible. Spirits and the Fae are attracted to children and are, in my opinion, often the cause of nightmares and the source of that particularly troublesome kind of imaginary friend who can drive a parent to despair. Children have a hard enough time growing up without us complicating the situation by waking up dormant genius loci. So, apart from a few transient brownies and other fairly harmless creatures stopping in from time to time, for the best part of seven years, my only interaction with the Fae was outdoors.

My daughter wasn't the only reason why I hadn't tried awakening this particular spirit. The house had a very strange energy and history about it, and as someone who truly believes that discretion is the better part of valor when it comes to working with the Fae, my gut was telling me that it was best to leave well enough alone. I had been drawn to the house straight away; it was quirky and unusual. Despite it being under offer for a considerable while for reasons that will never be entirely clear, I insisted that the agent make a viewing appointment. The minute I saw it, I knew I wanted the house. So, I wasn't surprised when just a few days later, the agent rang to say that the original offer had fallen through and the family wanted to give us first refusal.

Shortly after moving in, I started hearing the stories of the two families who had lived in the house previously. There were some very startling similarities to my own family setup. They were professional couples with a single child; the fathers worked away from home on a semiregular basis. In each case, the relationships broke down. The tales of the first family who moved in could have come straight out of Stephen King's *The Shining*, complete with the mother attempting to break down a door, behind which the husband was hiding with a

---

38. D. Morehouse, *Psychic Warrior: The True Story of America's Foremost Psychic Spy and the Cover-Up of the CIA's Top-Secret Stargate Program* (London: Clairview Publishing, 2004), 33–34.

large kitchen knife. Whatever guarded that house and its land, I did not want it becoming any more sentient than it already was.

It is often worthwhile in situations like this to have a little dig around to find out about the local area. In this case, much of the land was built on old mining property. There was even a covenant on the house that stated a "peppercorn" rent needed to be paid to the original landowners, who had retained all mineral rights in perpetuity. Basically, there was a mine under our house, and the folks who sold the land wanted to get rich off it if, for some reason, it were reopened. It became obvious that the lar or genius loci on this particular part of the land was a mining spirit, probably a bluecap or knocker of some kind. One who no longer served its original purpose and had found a way to adapt.

Bluecaps are known to manifest as blue flames. Already quite adapted to a life shared with humans, they are known for warning miners of impending shaft collapses. They were also said to aid in the workings of the mine. It was not surprising when I discovered that it had taken residence in the gas fireplace in the family lounge; it was the perfect location. Sadly, it was confused and not very aware of who or what it was and was definitely as much thought-form as it was urban Fae. Definitely a class 1, he had been woken by the heightened emotions of the first inhabitants of the house. Feeding off fear and anger, it continued to exist in a barely conscious state. This is one of the few times that I have chosen to adopt a policy of complete noninterference, and for the entire time I lived in that house, I worked very hard to keep the spirit dormant.

Before I moved out and made the property ready for rental, I made a conscious decision to remove the ancient metal fireplace and cap the gas supply that fed it in the hopes that the lar would relocate to somewhere more suitable, like back to the mine beneath the house. I did not want responsibility for anything that might befall my tenants. It was then with great horror that, after several months of the property sitting vacant, the only suitable tenants were a young professional couple with one child whose father worked away fairly regularly. The arguments, according to the neighbors, were monumental, and after they left a year or two later, I had to replace several doors and fill a number of holes in the plasterboard, which were obviously made by fists. It was the one and only time I banished a spirit, and although it gave me no joy, I truly believe it was the right thing to do to ensure no other young family suffered the same way.

ALIGNING YOURSELF WITH FIRE

While acclimatizing to the element of fire, you might like to scry with flames, eat fiery food with spicy or rich flavors, try meditation during a red sunset, and wear only fire colors.

· EXERCISE ·
finding the spirit of fire

The first part of this exercise is to find something made of fire. This is a slightly more challenging task, but a little bit of thought yields some interesting options. Unlike the other elements, it may not be possible to physically touch the essence of fire, but anything with a fiery aura is good enough. Possible items may be the following:

- A piece of pumice stone
- Smoke from a fire or incense
- A light bulb or candle flame (please make sure it doesn't get too hot; I don't want you burning yourself)
- A feng shui crystal reflecting sunlight

Pick a time when you aren't going to be disturbed for a while and spend a few minutes working with the verdant breath. Allow the spirit of ivy to cleanse your body and mind, preparing you for the work ahead.

Now, go one step further, and imagine yourself as the element of fire you are working with. Imagine what the flame or source feels when you touch. What energy is it sensing from you? Does your contact hurt, or is it pleasurable? If you were the flame, would you want to make contact, and why? It cannot be stressed enough that you need to trust your instincts and your imagination here. The more you use imagination, the better your connection will become.

CASE STUDY 2: THE GANCANAGH

In 2010, the YouTube vlogger and traditional witch George Hares was leaving work in the early hours of the morning when he was approached by an astonishingly attractive and well-dressed Irishman.[39] Initially, this didn't seem a strange occurrence; George worked in a nightclub in the Manchester gay village, and handsome well-dressed men were not an unusual occurrence. However, as soon as the man spoke, it became apparent that this situation was not normal. The man was very insistent in his desire to find women. To the point where he stalked and confronted George at multiple locations along George's route home, growing increasingly agitated at the lack of available women and at each point interacting with George as if he'd never spoken to him before.

This wasn't an isolated incident. Some years later, George decided to post his story on his YouTube channel; he received multiple comments telling similar tales of an inhumanly beautiful male intent on seeking out and connecting with women. The sightings were not confined just to the European continent, either. At a similar time, women on the North American continent were also reporting sightings. All the witnesses were lucky to escape with their lives—however, their hearts were not always so lucky.

The supernatural man easily fits into the species known as the gancanagh, or love-talker. Early folklore attributes these Fae with a shimmering glamour that allows them to adapt to their environment and appeal to the deepest desires of whomever they are trying to seduce. They are also supposed to exude a toxin from their skin that is both intoxicating and addictive; this toxin allegedly holds the victim in his thrall. He has always been quite comfortable approaching and interacting with humanity, for even the earliest tales speak of the gancanagh approaching campfires dressed in very recognizable human clothing of the era to listen to the dreams and desires of the females present before choosing his lover.

Considering his sinister intent and very present nature, he is most definitely a class 3 fully sentient Fae. Under the Aarne-Thompson-Uther Index, this particular faery would most definitely fall under the category of "supernatu-

---

39. G. Hares, "A run in with the Fairy (my terrifying experience) AMAZING STORY," YouTube, accessed October 30, 2019, https://www.youtube.com/watch?v=-BmM57PbdYA&t=12s.

ral adversary" along with vampires, seductive mere-maids, faery grooms who abduct their brides, and devilish Fae at crossroads.

· MEDITATION ·
journey to the spirit of fire

Allow your perception of the mundane world to slip quietly away. The image of reality dissolves and blows away like the wind. Mist swirls around you, gray, green, sickly yellow. It obscures your vision and numbs your senses. This mist hangs dense, forming condensation on your eyelids, your hair. Plumes of thick breath billow out in front of you. You feel deeply rooted in this place between places. Take a few moments to ensure you have fully immersed yourself in this other space. This is neither here nor there—a staging point to allow you to acclimatize. Breathe normally. There is nothing to fear.

The mist parts, dissipating almost as quickly as it arrived. You find yourself in a large room. It is four-sided, a square, and upon the floor are tiles of white marble and black onyx with a fabulous citrine dragon inlaid upon them. The north is directly in front of you, the south behind, east to your right, west to your left. Upon each wall is a brightly illustrated mural depicting various magickal creatures. Turning around toward the south, you face the image of a scarlet phoenix. You realize that this image is made up entirely of living flames and that the whole wall is a large fireplace.

Your heart beats quickly in your chest, and you can feel the essence of life and creativity flowing through your veins, pumping hope and power and ambition through you. The swoosh of blood in your ears is now layered with the crackle and roar of wild fire flickering and dancing, casting shadows upon the checkered floor. Take a deep breath and step into the fire.

The fire consumes you atom by atom in just an instant; you become nothing more than hot ash, which rushes up through the flue of the fireplace and out into a scorched landscape dyed vermilion by the large setting sun. There is a collection of primitive huts below you. One in particular draws your ashen self closer, for the heat that emanates from this place is far higher than any of the other buildings. You swirl and turn and coalesce back into your normal form and step inside what is obviously the village forge. But it's like no forge you have ever experienced before; the walls are lined not only with crude horseshoes and plowshares, but with objects wrought from the finest silver, so delicate they could make you cry with their beauty, and mechanisms whose functions you could not even hazard to guess.

The smith turns from their work to look at you. It's a startling sight, for the smith is a strong, muscular, and obviously pregnant woman—not what you were expecting at all. She laughs uproariously at your shock and introduces herself; she is called Cain. She beckons you forth to take a seat just beside her and stare into the flames of her forge. The coals glow hot and hypnotic. The images start to dance in front of your eyes: the first hominid wielding a flaming branch, the ability to keep out the dark, engines of war—all this is shown to you, and more. Allow it all to flow like molten lava, a fire on your head and in your mind, a hypnotic mix of inspiration and fear. From time to time between each scene, the coals spit, and creatures not of this realm dance in the center of each flickering light.

The flames eventually burn low. The coals are now just dying embers; Cain is sitting in almost darkness, waiting patiently for your return. She steps toward you, taking your hand and placing it on her distended belly. You feel the stirrings of the life she carries within. A tiny foot pushes against your palm, making you smile. Cain leans forward and kisses your forehead gently, and the world starts to dissolve around you. Moments later, you find yourself on the checkerboard floor once again. Take a moment; don't rush to return to reality just yet. This place is here to help you. When you are ready, call out and ask the mist to come carry you home to the here and now.

FINDING OTHER FAE

We have harnessed fire so thoroughly that finding Fae aligned with the element of fire should not be difficult in urban locations. Consider the following creatures when you come across any particular spirit that strikes you as a fire Fae.

IMPS—EUROPEAN COUNTERPARTS OF THE GENIE OR DJINN?

Much of the European folklore surrounding beings who are specifically named imp also considers them to be small devils, witch familiars, demons from hell, and so on. This heavy Christianizing is due mostly to the work of a fifteenth-century monk, Alphonso de Spina, who took the time to classify as many demons as he could discover. Many of his demons, however, were Fae folk, including goblins, a species that, according to de Spina, the imp belongs to. Online references claim that some imps can be bound to a bottle or a crystal or a glass, much like the genies in Arabic lore, and certainly they can, but so can a whole raft full of spirits if you are so inclined to put the work in. Hindu folklore tells of implike creatures who worked as attendants for the gods and goddesses of that pantheon. Some imps were good, and others worked for evil; they even had their own not-name name: the punya-janas, or good people. Considering the general opinion that Celtic lore was heavily influenced by Vedic mythology thanks to trade routes, these similarities are not surprising, and we may again be seeing a situation where a Fae has migrated with a particular culture—in this case, the Indo-Aryan people.

Their nature, whether good or evil, is inherently troublesome and tricky, but they are normally able to grant wishes. Therefore, it is possible to bargain and draw up a contract with an imp to have them become your familiar without having to do any binding whatsoever. They are very good at creating havoc and discord that serve as a catalyst for change, but they do have to be managed extremely carefully. Make sure you stick to any bargain you agree to should you discover an imp; as with many of the Fae, they are quick to turn against you if you don't honor your side of the deal.

JACK O' THE LANTERN AND JOAN THE WAD

Not all Fae given the title will-o'-the-wisp are the gaseous kind found in mines or marshes. The queen of the pixies in Cornwall is known as Joan the Wad. Both she and her partner, Jack o' the Lantern, are said to manifest as a light source. *Wad* is an Old Cornish word for a bundle of straw used as a makeshift torch. Jack and Joan can be invoked to help when you are lost or to illuminate a situation that is unclear to you. Stuck in a strange town and Google Maps isn't working? Is it late and you've got a long journey in foul weather? Try calling on Jack and Joan with the following traditional rhyme:

> *Jack o' the Lantern, Joan the Wad, who tickled the maid and made her mad,*
> *Light me home, the weather's bad.*[40]

---

40. Oxford Reference, "Joan the Wad," Oxford Reference, accessed November 21, 2019, https://
www.oxfordreference.com/view/10.1093/oi/authority.20110803100021143.

There are other regional variations of the idea of an indwelling Fae in human-made flame, such as Jack and Meg in the Wads, who are almost identical to Jack o' the Lantern and Joan the Wad, and Kit a Can Sticks, which, as the name suggests, is a fire sprite found in candle flames. Your local flame spirit may ask to be called something different once you get to know them.

A LAST WORD ON SALAMANDERS

In many of the Western mystery traditions, thanks to the early works of Paracelsus, the elements are still considered the realms of the following creatures: gnome for earth, undine for water, sylph for air, and salamander for fire. Salamanders are, in my opinion, mythical beasts, not Fae. They have their own folklore and mythology, including the ability to extinguish fires and make a human fire retardant, and basic meteorology skills to predict wet and dry weather.

Salamanders tend to just show up rather than respond to invocation, and in many ways, they can be considered the purest earthly incarnation of the element of fire. While scrying a flame, you may become aware of a small, almost reptilian creature crawling around within it, but their level of sentience is entirely different (not less) than that of fire Fae. If you are lucky enough to have a coal or woodstove in your home, it can be really handy to cultivate a salamander to look after your stove to ensure you don't have any chimney fires or problems lighting it. But don't expect a deep and meaningful conversation or any revelations regarding the otherworld, because that's not where the salamander dwells.

· EXERCISE ·
Graffiti scrying image activity

Use this image to practice elemental graffiti scrying (discussed in chapter 6).

Portal for the Element of Fire—Granada, Spain
Photographed by Tara Sanchez

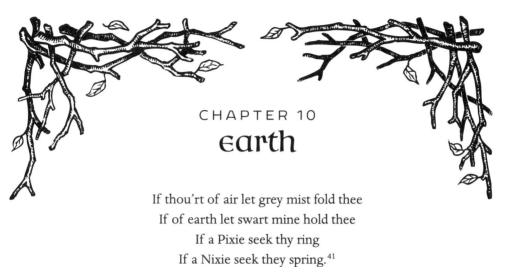

CHAPTER 10
earth

If thou'rt of air let grey mist fold thee
If of earth let swart mine hold thee
If a Pixie seek thy ring
If a Nixie seek they spring.[41]

The idea that humanity is somehow created from or connected to the earth is ubiquitous throughout world history. The ancient Egyptian god Khnum was said to fashion each human from clay on his potter's wheel before placing the child into its mother's womb. The Greek god Prometheus, in one of the many creation myths of that particular culture, made humans from dust and water and gave them fire. Some Indigenous American tribes hold that a creator spirit made humans from mud, letting them dry in the sun before breathing life into them. Even the God of Abraham and Allah were said to have made humanity from clay.

This common connection across world mythology is not entirely surprising, considering that, without the earth, we would not even exist. The right combination of organisms swimming around in a primordial goop of earth and water came together on the right day and life began. And what's more, we would not be the humans we are today had our agrarian societies not been possible; harnessing the land was a game changer, for evolution is much harder with an entirely hand-to-mouth existence. Therefore, you would assume that our easiest connection to the spirits of the other would be with those of the land; however, when it comes to modern sightings, this may not be the case. We can hypothesize why until we are blue in the face, but in reality, it is probably because the

---

41. W. Scott, *The Poetical Works of Walter Scott* (London: Houlston and Stoneman, 1848).

creatures associated with the element of earth are not portrayed as glamorously as other elemental spirits. As such, they are easier to dismiss when seen.

In Eastern philosophy, the element of earth is ruled by the planet Saturn and thought to correspond with the concepts of marriage and fertility, home, finances, and business. These correspondences are nearly the same in Western traditions. Earth is the essence of late summer and the harvest. Also, according to the five-element system, earth can include items such as bone and compostable substances that create soil, so while some plant divas will fall under the element of wood, some will fall under the element of earth. There is no hard-and-fast rule as to how to work this out, sadly, but time and practice will help you.

MODERN SIGHTINGS— THE SANTIAGO PARK PIXIE

In the early 2000s, a German photographer published a picture of a small figure walking as clear as day across an avenue in a public park in Santiago, Chile.[42] Although dubbed the Santiago Park Pixie by some, there is no evidence one way or another to suggest what type of Fae this actually was. Detractors have suggested that it was clever photo manipulation—very clever, considering the era in which the photo was published—and some have suggested it was a little dog leaping into the air, although how they came to this conclusion is anybody's guess, because it would have been the strangest-shaped dog ever.

The figure is approximately child-size when compared to the two mounted policemen who are also in the picture (apparently oblivious to this little being sharing the same space with them). The spirit is not dissimilar to the aliens known as grays—slightly elongated arms, legs, and head. There is a stoop to its posture suggesting age, but not infirmity, for its stride shows purpose—an adult gait, not the running skips of a child or dog.

Dwarflike figures and other little people are fairly common on both the North and South American continents with hundreds of sightings recorded in recent history, not to mention the oral tales of many Indigenous peoples from further back. These beings are often called duendes, just like the Zaragoza gob-

---

42. Camilo Valdivieso, "The Parque Forestal Humanoid Photograph—Santiago, Chile," Paranormal.lt, accessed November 2020, https://paranormal.lt/parque-forestal-humanoid-photograph.

lin, but most are neither domestic nor helpers, suggesting that they have taken the name but are another spirit altogether.

CASE STUDY 1: THE FROAD

My first case study is the froad. He is a quiet, unassuming little chap. Not particularly big, no particular skills, and he's definitely lost a battle or two with the ugly stick. In short, when I first came across him, he didn't know how to do much except sort of sit there, all boggle-eyed and squishy.

The froad—or, to give his full name, the fag toad—lived in an old cast-iron cauldron outside a guest house in Ireland. The cauldron was used by guests to dispose of their cigarette ends (fags). But, as is the case with these things, the cauldron was rarely emptied and often held vast quantities of black, sticky liquid thanks to frequent rainfall. I suspect that this little unlikely hero would have remained unnoticed until his eventual demise when his cauldron became so toxic that it needed to be emptied or thrown away completely, particularly because this supernatural creature was living in a home made from iron, the very thing that faery spirits are said to abhor—not a place one would normally go looking for the Fae. The whole guest house was hired out for an entire week by a raggle-taggle bunch of occultists, magicians, and witches for the purpose of performing magick together. A group uniquely placed to see things that normally go unseen.

And so it was as I sat one evening with a colleague partaking in the dreaded nicotine that I became aware of a pair of eyes peering curiously over the edge of the cauldron. I smiled and waved and pointed it out to my friend. So taken aback with fright was this poor little dude that he dived into his sludge and didn't reappear until several hours later. This time there were more of us on the veranda where his humble abode stood, and we questioned him, asking him for his name. He didn't really know what his name was, other than froad, and language skills were not a strong point.

This friendly chap revealed through broken imagery that he didn't remember a life "before," so we can only surmise that he came into existence sometime in the latter half of 2004, about six months after the smoking ban was enforced in Ireland, although I didn't make his acquaintance until 2007. But as the week went by and twenty-five magickal people essentially filled him full of energy, he grew more confident and came out to say hello with increasing regularly. By the end of the week, he managed to communicate to one of the group that he was worried his cauldron was too full. We had already discussed his now numerous and obvious appearances and the trouble those might cause when we left, so one of the members took him home (with his excited permission) in a small jar containing some of his sticky tar-water so he could make a new place to live. He remains there happily to this day.

The froad is a class 1 spirit. He is more thought-form than actual Fae. He may have started out life as something more natural and coherent or even as a misplaced spirit, like a bluecap, but his corruption is so far gone that he has no recollection of who or what he was before. He has only maintained a foothold in this world by becoming something else entirely with the aid of the beliefs and energy of humans.

It took me a long time to come to terms with the fact that the froad was primarily an earth-based Fae (designated water of earth). Everything in my system screamed that he should be either fire, because tobacco is martial and fiery, or air, because air is a mental stimulant and smoky. But this is a common trap to fall into. My husband often shakes his head and exclaims in exasperation, "You're anthropomorphizing again!" And he's right. I so often want to find meaning or significance based on my own world and perceptions. I have decades of indoctrination that tell me why tobacco ought to be associated with either fire or air; after all, if that's in all the books, then it must be right, surely. Wrong!

Froad's origins, without doubt, lie in the idea of a plant diva. A spirit of the tobacco plant itself. Each and every cigarette smoked and discarded into the cauldron contained a small amount of the leaves of the tobacco plant. Shredded, processed, and abused through burning though it may have been, a small part of the original essence remained, one far more akin to the earthly realms than any other.

ALIGNING YOURSELF WITH EARTH

While you are working with the spirit of earth, you may like to consider the following activities to gain a well-rounded understanding. Try working with clay or gardening, eating only earth-related foodstuffs (such as root vegetables and unprocessed meats), wearing only earth colors, and walking barefoot in the mud.

· EXERCISE ·
ꝼinðing the spirit oꝼ earth

Find something made of earth that has been manufactured or shaped by human hands. This shouldn't present too much of a problem. It needs to be either small enough to hold in your hands or in a position that you can sit comfortably on it, against it, or with your hands touching it for a reasonable period of time. Possible items may be the following:

- A pottery cup or plate
- A handful of potting compost (stuff that has been seriously processed)
- An antique bone hair ornament or pendant
- A piece of brick or cinder block

Pick a time when you aren't going to be disturbed for a while. Spend a few minutes working with the verdant breath. Allow the spirit of ivy to cleanse your body and mind, preparing you for the work ahead. Feel the item and its essence, and then imagine the item feeling you. Review the other elemental exercises for more guidance on this process.

CASE STUDY 2: ROUVARIA OF THE LAMIA

Lamias are well-known faeries. They have a long provenance with documented stories as far back as ancient Greece. A few stories suggest that the lamia are terrifying monsters, while others portray them as half maiden, half serpent or dragon. The early Greek myths state that the original Lamia was one of Zeus's many lovers who was driven mad by Hera, who murdered Lamia's children and took away her ability to sleep. Zeus took pity on the poor girl and gave her the ability to remove her eyes and to shape-shift. And, it seems, the ability to procreate, as tales of the lamia range across all of Europe, Africa, and the Middle East, many being found in urban environments.

One very famous lamia was said to have owned a fabulous house in the richest quarter of Corinth. It was an amazing structure decked out in silks and fineries and complete with servants. She was known for hosting extravagant parties for the handsome young men who took her fancy. Sadly, this association with luxury was not to last, and over time lamias became more impoverished, living in bawdy drinking establishments and hovels, likened more to the haglike witches who became very popular thanks to Roman satirists. Even

later myths denigrate them further, suggesting they are more akin to suc-
cubi than anything else, preying upon and sucking the life force from the very
same young, unsuspecting men whom she was said to have courted in ancient
Greece. Regardless of their fall from grace, it is clear that lamias have always
roamed among us even in the earliest times, and they acclimatized to living
with humans fairly rapidly. They have been a class 3 spirit pretty much from
the get-go, and that doesn't seem likely to change.

I started working with Rouvaria at the request of a magickal colleague.
They sent me a shabby, smelly, and very dated gentleman's briefcase decorated
with snakeskin. It was truly horrible. Worse still, it was locked, and no key was
with the parcel, just a request to investigate the object. They had found it in
a house clearance sale and had felt compelled to purchase it. I couldn't even
imagine why somebody would want to send me such a thing, let alone suggest
it had any kind of magickal essence about it. I threw it into the boot of my
car, refusing to have the ghastly thing in my house. My intention was to take
it to the municipal waste site at the earliest opportunity. But something always
transpired to stop me from making the journey!

Eventually, it became apparent that I wasn't ever going to be allowed to
take the revolting thing to the dump until I had solved its riddle. So, out of
the car it came. I had no desire to open the case without first trying to ascer-
tain what was inside the dratted thing, so I began a long set of explorations.
Initially, I went through weeks of dowsing and divination, assuming that the
unease I sensed around the item may have been related to legal documents,
wills, or contracts with nefarious intent. But I could confirm nothing. It was as
if my skills had failed me. That in its own right suggested to me there was even
more to this than met the eye. Next, I meditated with the case, sitting with
it upon my lap, hands placed lightly on the top, sensing what may be inside.
Again, I could sense nothing. So, I threw caution to the wind and jimmied the
locks open with a screwdriver. Nothing. Empty—not even a scrap of paper or a
dried Biro, so what on earth was I sensing?

I felt that the snakeskin was probably the key to the puzzle, as that appeared
to have the most "energy" surrounding it, so, over the course of several sessions, I started the process of waking up whatever was inherent in the skin.
Honestly, as I type this, I would not blame you if you believed I was mad,
because I would. But slowly over time, I became aware of a very sleepy, very
subdued spirit. I meditated and journeyed with it, left it offerings of milk and

honey, and even invoked several deities responsible for memory in the hopes that I could get some clear idea as to what this creature was.

She was a lamia, and her name was Rouvaria—or at least that is how it sounded to me, and she never corrected me. But as we already know, that isn't uncommon for the Fae. Years later, I came across *The Grimoire of Arthur Gauntlett*: an amazing collection of spells, seals, charms, and invocations from the seventeenth century, including the invocation of seven faery sisters, one of which was named Rouvaria. Without a shadow of a doubt, this lamia was one and the same.

How she had become trapped in the case has never been entirely clear. It is possible she was placed there by a Fae worker or magician at an earlier time, but it just seemed too far-fetched. Seriously, what were the odds of a magickal item in the guise of a 1970s snakeskin briefcase making its way into not one, but two magickal practitioners' hands, the latter of which was also a Fae worker?

I believe the more plausible answer is that she was unsuccessfully invoked by a grimoire magician, leaving her to wander in a state of confusion, and then summarily banished from another location by said magician or by an overzealous person worried about things that go bump in the night. In the metaphysical shunt, she ended up fragmented and in the vicinity of said briefcase, which felt at least a little energetically aligned thanks to the snakeskin. Like all wounded creatures, humans included, she crawled into the nearest quiet, dark location and went dormant until she felt better, which, considering her state, may well have been never if I hadn't intervened. Once I had ascertained that she was an earth-based lamia, the awakening process was quite simple. Lamia, like their sisters the melusines and the empusa, are creatures of glamor and comfort. Simple offerings of flowers, chocolates, wine, incense, and energy (in this case, taking the time to draw an image of her, which was eventually offered up to flames once she was ready to move on) was enough to get her up and running again.

Please picture this in your darkest moments, for it will surely raise a smile: a tacky plastic briefcase placed lovingly upon an altar, candles burning, incense rising, charcoals glowing, libations of milk and honey before it, and one young Druidish witch muttering words of invocation and love. I hope in ten thousand years' time this fragment of my book survives and confuses the heck out of an archaeologist, because to this day, it still confuses the heck out of me! But in return for restoring her to health, I was assured that should I ever need her help, I just had to call on her again, and one of her sisters would aid me. I have only done this once: assistance in a spell to shield me with her glamour from the unwanted attentions of an online nuisance.

Note: Some tales do suggest that the lamia is a succubus—essentially a vampiric spirit. Be very careful about how you broker any energy exchange with one of these spirits should you encounter one.

· MEDITATION ·
journey to the spirit of earth

Allow your perception of the mundane world to slip quietly away. The image of reality dissolves and blows away like the wind and mist swirls around you—gray, green, sickly yellow. It obscures your vision and numbs your senses. This mist hangs dense, forming condensation on your eyelids, in your hair. Plumes of thick breath billow out in front of you. You feel deeply rooted in this place between places. Take a few moments to ensure you have fully immersed yourself in this other space. This is neither here nor there—a staging point to allow you to acclimatize. Breathe normally. There is nothing to fear.

The mist parts, dissipating almost as quickly as it arrived. You find yourself in a large room. It is four-sided, a square, and upon the floor are tiles of white marble and black onyx with a fabulous citrine dragon inlaid upon them. The north is directly in front of you, the south behind, the east to your right, the west to your left. Upon each wall is a brightly illustrated mural depicting various magickal beasts. Kneel down and touch the image of the citrine dragon. Feel the lines where the semiprecious stones intersect with the ceramic tiles buzzing against your fingertips with the energy of the earth from whence they came.

Your heart beats slowly in your chest, and the dragon slowly starts to rotate around you. Pinned to the center, you feel full of potential and radiant like the sun: the very essence of summer. The swoosh of blood in your ears is now layered with the sound of a ripe harvest crop rippling in the breeze, cattle lowing in a field some distance away, and children playing. You are filled with hope and warmth. The dragon spins faster until you can no longer make out its physical shape—a blur of wheaten gold, pulsing and shifting. Take a deep breath and cry, "Stop!"

The spinning stops and you find yourself crouched in the center of a giant golden lotus flower. The landscape around you is split into two distinctly different parts: one side is full and rich and verdant, the other barren and dry. At the boundary between these two realms stands a solitary figure; he is short, bearded, and covered in spiraling tattoos in white, black, and red. He introduces himself to you; his name is Emrys, and he is your guide along this journey. Beckoning toward you, Emrys offers you a bowl of sweet nectar to drink. You are parched, for the sun beats down from above and burns your head, but you refuse, knowing that drinking would tether you to this place and time against your will.

As you stand with Emrys, you realize that here on the boundary you can see the world around you turning slowly; civilizations are rising and falling. Abundant harvests flourish and desolate crop failures cause widespread famine. With each age, there is a wise one, a magician, a lawmaker who joins you at the boundary, controlling the events, maintaining the balance between life and death before disappearing to allow another to take their place. To each age there is born a wise one, a gift to the world capable of walking between both realms. Let events unfold around you. Allow the images to show you what you need to know. Lessons from the element of earth.

Eventually, you realize there is no more you can absorb as part of this journey. Perhaps next time you will see and understand more. Sighing, you thank Emrys for your gift and step back inside the lotus. Your vision darkens momentarily, and you find yourself on the checkerboard floor once again. Don't rush to return to reality just yet; this place is here to help you adjust, to process. When you are ready, call out and ask the mist to carry you home, to the here and now.

....

FINDING OTHER FAE

The following are other Fae whom you may readily find in urban locations. Although they may come from very specific locations around the world, you will find their relatives in cities, towns, and suburban environments near you. Therefore, it is worth learning a little something about these Fae and how you can work with them, which will aid you when you come across any particular spirit who strikes you as an earth Fae.

THE BOGGART

There are many stories regarding the boggart, some of which suggest that boggarts were once good brownies who have since gone bad.[43] Therefore, it would be easy to categorize them as domestic helper spirits (discussed in the section on wood). However, in Northwest England alone, there are dozens of recorded place names associated with boggarts, many of which still have folklore attached to them. There are railway boggarts, bridge boggarts, cave boggarts, house boggarts, and even a boggart that has its own brewery. Probably the most famous boggart in the UK is the boggart of Boggart Hole Clough. This was an invisible but mischievous spirit who attached itself to a family living on a local farm. The manifestation became so bad that the family decided they would rather starve than remain in the farmhouse any longer, packing all their belongings onto a horse and cart and heading into town. En route, they came across a neighbor who inquired as to where they were going. A little voice from the back shouted out, "We's doin' a flit; they don't like it back there." The farmer, realizing the futility of escape, turned the cart for home.

Different versions of this story exist, but there are some common themes through each tale. The first is that this Fae was always a boggart; there was no transformation from disgruntled brownie to boggart. Second, he was not specifically attached to one location, being prepared to move with the family into town, which suggests that he could become bonded to a family. Some tenuous folklore about a specific boggart suggests that it is the naming of the Fae that binds it to the family; this illustrates how important it is to really know what you are working with and also how important names are.

It would be a fundamental mistake to buy into the concept of the disgruntled brownie as it would do the boggart a great disservice. Boggarts are beings in their own right and worthy of investigation. They are happy to live in and around humanity, as their historical tales suggest. They aren't always inherently helpful, nor are they tied to any organic, living item. They feel far more earthy and of the earth, with so many of them dwelling outdoors even in urban locations. The boggart species may well have emigrated abroad with settlers and

---

43. J. Harland and T. Wilkinson, *Lancashire Folk-lore Illustrative of the Superstitious Beliefs and Practices, Local Customs and Usages of the People of the County Palatine* (London: Frederick Warne & Co., 1867), 49–50.

taken on the name bogie, bogart, or boogie, so when looking for local lore to track down any in your area, consider searching for those names as well.

Boggarts can be petitioned for help once contact has been made, but they're not very reliable, and once you start paying them, they can get quite annoying and troublesome if you stop. They are better cultivated as the guardian Fae of that area, protecting it and, with your help, caring for it. In return, they may choose from time to time to impart interesting dreams, meditations, and a bit of lore, which tends to be easily verified when researched. In theory, if they become a nuisance, they can be warded off with either ash or bay laurel. Another famous boggart, the Grizlehurst Boggart, was "laid to rest" either under an ash or a bay laurel tree; I have never needed to test this theory.

KORRIGANS AND DWARFS

Korrigans are a particular kind of dwarf associated with the amazing stone avenues in the French town of Carnac. Ti Goriquet, as it is known in the Breton language, is composed of more than four thousand standing stones, and according to local folklore, the ancient monument is the work of the little folk. Every night, they dance around the stones and drag unsuspecting travelers into their revelry until they drop with exhaustion. Each morning, the little men disappear with the dawn. They are sometimes known to sing songs, but be very careful how you join in. If you disturb the rhythm of the "cant," you could be subject to a curse.

As a rule, most dwarfs in myth and legend seem to be quite ambivalent to humanity unless you break one of their rules or taboos, such as spoiling the rhythm of their songs. But there are some who are less amicable and border on being a trickster or even a harbinger, like the Nain Rouge, which dwell in the Michigan area of the United States, particularly in the city of Detroit. This spirit, it is said, was once a guardian of the land, a peacemaker who coexisted with humanity until the founder of Detroit, Antoine de Cadillac, came across the dwarf one evening and, appalled by his ugly appearance, beat him with a stick, chasing him from the land.

The destruction of the truce between humans and spirits of place resulted in a metamorphosis of the Nain Rouge into an evil, twisted trickster who appears only during times of bloodshed and strife, or maybe the strife appears because of him. Reports of his involvement have spanned history, including the War of Independence in the 1700s, the Great Detroit Fire in the 1800s, the uprisings and riots in the 1900s, and now in the twenty-first century, he appears to be more brazen than ever before, breaking into cars and hanging out in bars and on city streets with little care as to if he is seen.

His tale is noteworthy for two reasons. First, he is the best example of why banishing a faery without a good reason is a fail of the most epic proportions. That casual beating given by de Cadillac not only left de Cadillac to die in poverty, but an entire city has now been haunted, for lack of a better word, for about three hundred years. Second, like the boggart in England, the Nain Rouge has been adopted by the citizens in the area in which he dwells, which is probably the reason his appearances are growing in number. He has a brewery, a red wine, and even a parade in his honor. That's a lot of energetic belief feeding his evolution into the modern world.

INA PIC WINNA

Lucy Cooper mentions this Fae in her most excellent book *An Encyclopedia of Faeries*, as does Katherine Briggs in her earlier seminal work *A Dictionary of Faeries* from the 1970s, although I believe they may have drawn from the same fragmentary lore, as there is little more written about this spirit. This Fae seems to be a land wight that has possibly taken on the name of an ancient tribal king named King Ina. What is curious about this particular Fae is that, over time, it built for itself a tradition of building cairns.

This is not an unusual phenomenon, and we will look at it a little more closely in chapter 12. For now, it is worth mentioning that any public parks or areas that have organically started to collect stone stacks, or even areas where the town planning suddenly has a fondness for modern "rock art," may be the result of an earth Fae's influence. The recorded lore regarding Ina Pic Winna claimed that the local fishermen would pick up a piece of white quartz on their way down to the boats before each journey and place it carefully on the cairn associated with this Fae. They would also chant, "Ina Pic Winna, send me a good dinner." It was believed that they would then return with an excellent haul. This is a perfect example of where you can use the literal nature of a Fae to aid you in a specific task. The fishermen did not just want to eat when they petitioned the local land spirit; their entire livelihood depended on the value of their catch, but it was recognized that a land spirit would have little understanding of the nature of human money. Therefore, keeping the intent as simple as possible ensured that there was no confusion and little chance for the Fae to play a trick. We can also use this technique when working with the Fae; it can be surprisingly effective.

· EXERCISE ·

Graffiti scrying image activity

You may like to use this image to practice elemental graffiti scrying (discussed in chapter 6).

Portal for the Element of Earth—Edinburgh, UK
Photographed by Tara Sanchez

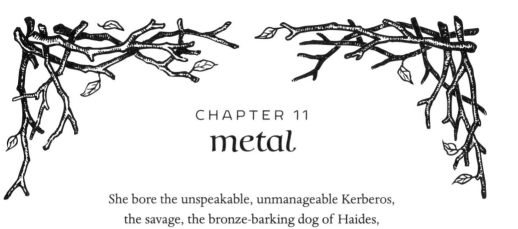

CHAPTER 11
metal

She bore the unspeakable, unmanageable Kerberos,
the savage, the bronze-barking dog of Haides,
fifty-headed, and powerful, and without pity.[44]

When this book first came into being as a half-formed idea, a collection of personal notes, and anecdotes by colleagues, all screaming to be organized and set free on the unsuspecting public, I had not yet started entertaining the idea of an extended hybrid elemental system. It was the spirits in the case studies of this chapter that led me to many hours of contemplation and investigation. Eventually, they were the catalyst of change within my personal philosophy regarding the Fae I was encountering with alarming regularity but who did not fit within the normal systems of classification.

Unsurprisingly, when researching modern sightings or myths associated with the element of metal, it was almost impossible at first to find examples. Even the most mundane of people in the Western world tend to use the classical four-element system when explaining supernatural encounters. Then it struck me that many trickster spirits are essentially mercurial and therefore metallic in nature. Also, the constant tales of iron being repugnant, even fatal, to the Fae have caused us to be blinkered to how we look at the Fae and how they interact with metallic substances. It's all too easy to discount every kind of metal as a result, which is why I suspect the hybrid elemental classification used in this book has gone pretty much unnoticed. But once you get past this, other Fae who seem to have an affinity to metallurgy or smithwork start becoming apparent and may also need to be reclassified as you come across them, such as

---

44. Hesiod, "Theogony," translated by Evelyn-White, Theoi, accessed October 2019, https://
    www.theoi.com/Ther/KuonKerberos.html.

Rumpelstiltskin, who spun straw into gold; Alviss, a dwarfish master smith in Norse mythology; and, of course, there are always exceptions to the iron rule if you recall our little froad in chapter 10 who lived in a cast-iron pot.

Within Eastern philosophy, the element of metal is thought to correspond with the concepts of leadership, governance, alliances, creativity, children, and success. It is also aligned with what we might consider destructive energies, such as banishment, cursing, severing ties, and binding. It is the essence of autumn, the end of expansive fertility. Many of these aspects are that which we would normally associate with elemental fire in Western traditions. But if you think carefully, this makes perfect sense. Most of humanity's major developments, including war, law, education, and science, have occurred because of their manipulation and control of metal. The Greek philosopher Hesiod even split our development into five ages, four of which corresponded to metallic substances.

During the Golden Age, humankind lived to be incomprehensibly old but kept a youthful appearance, even in death. They talked freely with the animals and the gods alike. This is actually slightly more complicated than it appears, in that this was "human version 1.0," which may or may not have been our actual ancestors at all. It's more likely, considering their attributes, that they were High Fae, or sídhe. But thanks to some of the usual infighting among the Greek gods, many of the Men of Gold died, and those who remained ended up wandering the world as benevolent spirits in subsequent generations, and maybe even to this day.

The next age was called the Age of Silver. Here, the gods had a go at creating "human version 1.1." This didn't end well for this species either. They were foolish and took hundreds of years to mature. The gods found them irritating and irreverent, and they destroyed them all in a rage. The destruction of the Men of Silver, however, was only physical, and they were sent to the underworld to become the spirits of Hades. It's worth remembering that at that point, Hades had not been split into different regions, such as the fields of Ashphodel, Tartarus, or Elysium, so all spirits, either dead or just incarcerated, wandered together. It was possible to escape this realm if you knew what you were doing or had the right connections.

The Men of Bronze, "human version 1.2," were an absolute disaster for the gods, all things considered. They were warriors with wrathful and destructive personalities. What is curious is that ancient texts suggest they turned to cannibalism and very significantly "rejected bread," which, considering the dislike of bread as an offering by some of the Fae, suggests that the Fae may well be some kind of descendant of this race of creatures created by the gods.

The Age of Heroes is most definitely the dawning of "human 2.0"; these beings are almost definitely the ancestors of humanity. They were considered demigods and were imbued with supernatural powers. This race undoubtedly would have had the ability to interact with beings from the previous incarnations, and this may be where many of our folktales and stories originated from, particularly as academics are now estimating that some fairy tales, such as Jack and the Beanstalk and Rumpelstiltskin, are between two and six thousand years old.

Hesiod declared that he lived in the Age of Iron, and we haven't progressed any further since. According to Hesiod, during this age, humans live an existence of toil and misery. Children dishonor their parents, family feuds cause deep rifts, the concepts and contracts of hospitality are forgotten. Might makes right, and bad people use lies to be thought good. Rather an alarming description of the worst part of our world today, so a few thousand years haven't improved our characters much, sadly.

The Reverend Kirk may have gotten his inspiration from this very idea, for he talked a fair amount about the sleagh maith (the good crowd). These were a species of beings who could be placed somewhere between angels and humanity, much akin to the Men of Gold in many respects. This, of course, is only one possible theory as to the origins of the good folk, but it is an excellent illustration of how strongly metal plays a role in the development of both humankind and beings who are other than human.

MODERN SIGHTINGS— THE PHANTOM BLACK DOG

The picturesque town of Todmorden in West Yorkshire has many reasons to be famous. In its time, it has hosted the rather dramatic mind experiments of the mentalist Derren Brown, harbored the serial killer Harold Shipman, and been the location of one of the biggest UFO frenzies ever to sweep the UK. To say there is something peculiar about the place is a bit of an understatement. One of the lesser-known supernatural celebrities in the area is a being

known as Old Scraper, a shape-shifting being who sometimes takes the form
of a phantom hound and appears at night to anyone brave enough to wander
the roads heading up to the ridgeline above the valley, brandishing their tools.
If he favors them and they can afford to pay, they wake up in the morning with
all their tools sharpened. A similar tale is told of the smith Wayland in Oxford-
shire; if you leave tools or your horse in need of new shoes along with a silver
coin, Wayland will perform the task unseen during the night, a skill, it is said,
he learned from the dwarfs.

The black dog is a common modern sighting often with an affinity for
metal, even iron.[45] For example, in 1981, a well-known talk show host in Guatemala fascinated his audience with a chilling tale.[46] Reported to have taken place
in the Cerrito del Carmen area of Guatemala City, he told of a mule driver and
his companion who, having decided to stop for the night, started drinking. The
mule driver became aware that his companion was significantly more sober
than he was despite matching him drink for drink, and he finally observed his
companion quietly pouring his drinks out.

Slightly obnoxious from drink, the mule driver, who was named Ceferino
Escobar, challenged his colleague about his actions. The poor man confessed
that he never drank in the city for fear of seeing the cadejo, a fearsome black
hound with goat hooves for feet; tall, rabbitlike ears; and glowing red eyes the
size of dinner plates. Escobar jeered and taunted this man for a superstitious
fool and coaxed and shamed him into drinking. The night passed, and they
became increasingly more inebriated to the point that they no longer knew
where they were. Tired, they lay down to rest under some trees at the side of
the street to sleep the heavy night off.

Many hours later, they woke, aching, dehydrated, heads pounding, and,
bizarrely, with Escobar's clothes in tatters as if ripped by the claws of a large,
predatory beast. Deciding that the only sensible course of action was to round
up their mules and head off for a proverbial "hair of the dog," they slowly
started their day. As they did so, they realized that one of the mules was missing, and they set about searching for it. Farther down the street, outside the
nearest bar, they found it safely tied. The bar owner had found it wandering

45. B. Trubshaw, *Explore Phantom Black Dogs* (UK: Heart of Albion Press, 2005).

46. S. Burchell, *Phantom Black Dogs in Latin America* (Leicestershire, UK: Heart of Albion Press,
2007).

and decided to keep it safe. When Escobar thanked him, the owner said, "It's a good thing, too. A madman escaped the asylum last night and was running around slashing at everything in sight. He would have killed you two sleeping under that tree had it not been for the large black dog that sat protecting your friend all night!"

After this, Escobar never teased anyone for believing in the supernatural and was known to leave offerings at the crossroads for el cadejo.

Most black dog spirits should be considered metal elemental spirits, for they are regularly reported as dragging large chains around their necks. They are also associated with buried treasure and even mines, something they share with their European counterpart. Across Europe, the black dog is often considered a harbinger and sometimes a protector of an area, a family, or a person; this also parallels its roles in Latin America. And our connection to this noble beast can be the same. They can warn us of impending doom, protect our homes and family, and even be petitioned to be a kind and gentle psychopomp when our passing or that of our loved one is upon us. They can even help us with information regarding legal matters.

Whether black dogs are truly Fae is up for debate, just like the salamander, but to that I would say, in what book does it state that the faeries have to be in humanoid form? Folktales are actually riddled with shape-shifting supernatural spirits that are almost always some kind of trickster or helper, or both! And many of the most famous interactions with faery kings and queens are heralded by the arrival of a supernatural creature. The King of the Wild Hunt, Gwyn ap Nudd, has a spectral hound called Dormach who rides into battle with him and also acts as a psychopomp.

While some hypothesize that many of the black dog stories in the Americas are a result of immigrant migration from Europe, there always seems to be another Indigenous story for the migrating Fae to latch on to, which suggests that the evolution of Fae is not a new thing. Our classifications are only new in the sense that we have named the Fae for the first time.

CASE STUDY 1: THE HOWK

I still have no actual given name for this creature, and quite possibly I never will, for I am not sure he remembers what his name once was. He is, in my opinion, a class 1 feral entity, and he lives in the drystone wall of a tumbledown outbuilding of an old bobbin mill in the Lake District. The outbuilding was a store in which chemicals used in the manufacturing process of the wooden bobbins were housed, and it never served any higher purpose than that, nor was it ever inhabited by humans, which may have activated a dormant nature spirit. But I suspect the fear and respect the workers felt toward these potentially fatal chemicals built up inside the granite drystone walls along with the fumes from the chemicals themselves and awoke something older and more primal within the stones, which fused with the thought-form that the workers were inadvertently creating.

I had traveled with some companions to visit the site at the suggestion of a regular visitor who cared for some more nature-based spirits deeper into the valley. The intention was, of course, to work with these natural spirits rather than look for any Fae in the old industrial part of the site. As normal, I asked to stop at a shop on the way to purchase boiled sweets and toffees as gifts. If there is one commonality among the Fae, be they feral or unchanged, it is a love of tobacco and candy. You can never go too far wrong if you go out on an adventure with those in your pockets. I was very close to the checkout when I had an overwhelming desire to buy Pontefract cakes, a form of sweet liquorice. I was very curious as to why the Fae I was visiting might want these items, as they weren't a normal offering; so, too, was my host, who had never given liquorice as an offering before. At the time, we could only conclude that it would be needed as a special offering.

As we approached the mill itself, our guide informed us that we would have to cross the wheelhouse and into the ravine behind. Opting to spend a few moments exploring the ruins, I found myself drawn to the outhouse, a forlorn place with no roof, the entrance barred by high-standing weeds. I carefully cleared the weeds and was instantly presented with the phenomenon of pareidolia. The head and shoulders of a male sprang out at me through the lichen and crumbling rock. Curious, I spent time looking at it, asking my companions to go on ahead without me.

Thanks to the fairly remote location and the overgrown nature of the outbuilding, I was content that any disturbance would come only from a curious dog out with its owner for a walk, and I settled in to see if I could make any contact. I allowed my breathing to settle, and, defocusing my eyes, I let my head drop so that I was not looking directly at the image in the rock. I sent out a gentle nudge to the being I called the howk, after the location we were visiting. I managed to glean just one word from this sleepy being: *arsenic*. It wasn't hard for me to work out that this was a substance that was kept in the stores, but what for? Why was that the only verbalization I could get from the howk? It's very simple; when cotton bobbins were made of wood, they were treated with a solution of copper salts and arsenic to prevent rotting, both of which are metallic compounds. It then became apparent that I was meant to leave the liquorice for this spirit. So, I placed the treats down on the ground, thanked the spirit, and walked away.

It would be nice to say that this Fae had a use or a practice that I learned and could pass on, but he is a very good example of a spirit of place who just is. A nice encounter with a sleepy entity doing nobody any harm at all. Something to be enjoyed and remembered fondly, just like a nice conversation with a stranger on the bus whom you know you will never see again.

ALIGNING YOURSELF WITH METAL

You may wish to augment this alignment further by working with metal materials, wearing metallic colors, eating only metal-related foods (such as substances naturally high in iron, magnesium, zinc, and calcium), using only metal implements to cook with, or sleeping and meditating with metals.

· EXERCISE ·
finding the spirit of metal

The first part of this exercise is to find something made of metal; this really shouldn't be too hard, as pretty much everything nowadays has some kind of metal component. It needs to be either small enough to hold in your hands or positioned so that you can sit comfortably on it, against it, or with your hands touching it for a reasonable period of time. I would be tempted to start with everyday metals, such as gold, silver, and iron. Possible items may be the following:

• A piece of gold or silver jewelry
• A cast or forged item, such as a spanner or wrench

- A metal garden chair
- A pressed steel pencil or sweet tin

As with the previous elements, it would be wise to pick a time when you aren't going to be disturbed for a while. Start by spending a few minutes working with the verdant breath. Allow the spirit of ivy to cleanse your body and mind, preparing you for the work ahead, and then start to feel your chosen object. Remember to make this a sensory, intuitive, and intellectual activity to really get a feel for every aspect of the item you are working with.

CASE STUDY 2: JON THE RUST SPIRIT

Jon is a spirit whom I have not met personally, although his likeness to the froad is undeniable. His story, just like that of the gancanagh, is so compelling I can only conclude that it is true. The way my informant worked with this spirit over a sustained period of time is impressive, and when she heard of this book, she sent me an eight-page, three-thousand-word document detailing her work. The following is a retelling based on her journal from 2005. For professional reasons, she asked not to be named and, therefore, shall be referred to as Jane.

Having landed a job for a charity providing treatment services to drug and alcohol users, Jane had moved to the busy city center of Sunderland in the North of England. Her job was to provide harm reduction and psychosocial interventions to addicts.

Sunderland was at that time (and to some extent still is) a strange dichotomy. The council was spending serious money to improve the part of the city center where her offices were based by constructing lit fountains, swanky apartments, and trendy bars, but on the other side of the street from this apparent luxury were bail hostels, used syringes, and evidence of poverty and deprivation hard to imagine in a Northern European city.

The office was by a four-way crossroads and adjacent to a pub. Between the building's front door and the pub, there was a joining wall about the width of two or three bricks. On that in-between wall, there was a metal box covering the office's shutter lock, a metal drain coming down from the roof, and, most importantly, a very old, grubby, and rusty ashtray.

Upon arriving early on her first day, Jane came into contact with the spirit she eventually would come to know as Jon. A sensation as if she had walked backward into someone came over her, and all her excitement and first-day jitters drained from her body. When she turned her head back, expecting to see a tall, broad male only to discover that no one was there, she immediately knew that she had come into contact with a spirit from the other. This strange presence persisted for several months, making itself known to her as she gained access and egress to the building. A presence that initially she tried to ignore, believing it to be a restless spirit of a deceased person.

The spirit, however, was quite persistent and started bombarding Jane with strange and unusual images, things that she didn't initially understand. Until, thanks to a series of circumstances, one of the images proved to be about an eventually troublesome member of staff whom she had not yet met. It was a warning, one that she didn't ignore. Her attitude changed, and she started acknowledging the spirit Jon, who was most definitely a class 2 spirit, for further work revealed partial memory connections to the spirit of the opium poppy, which did pass through the docks in Sunderland hundreds of years ago, and then persisted when crime and drug abuse grew in the area.

Unable to leave any traditional offerings as it was on a main road—all cemented pavement and office buildings—Jane started giving energetic offerings instead, rubbing her hands together and providing the warmth as a form of gratitude. Jon was not interested at all. He had chosen, like the froad, to take residence in a rusty ashtray outside the building and was happily feeding off the energy provided by gossip, anxiety, stress, and even intoxication from the workers and patients at the dependency clinic. With the ability to feed off the emotions of the city streets, one woman's gentle offerings of warmth were small potatoes in comparison.

Although his residence was in decay, just like Bar-El's, Jon didn't seem to be very concerned about this. Jane did talk to him regarding this several times over the four years she worked at that location. In many ways, he had embodied the spirit of rust as much as he had the opium poppy, and he was very comfortable with the idea of eventual decay and dissolution. Or evolution, depending on the way you look at it. After years of interviewing other Fae workers who choose to interact with urban and domestic spirits, this is something that is becoming increasingly common. For some of the Fae, there is now an idea of evolution, of transitioning to something else. I believe that it is our duty to allow that to happen when we come across it and even to aid when we are asked.

· M E D I T A T I O N ·
journey to the spirit of metal

Allow your perception of the mundane world to slip quietly away. The image of reality dissolves and blows away like the wind; mist swirls around you, gray, green, sickly yellow. It obscures your vision and numbs your senses. This mist hangs dense, forming condensation on your eyelids, in your hair. Plumes of thick breath billow out in front of you. You feel deeply rooted in this place between places. Take a few moments to ensure you have fully immersed yourself in this other space. This is neither here nor there—a staging point to allow you to acclimatize. Breathe normally. There is nothing to fear.

The mist parts, dissipating almost as quickly as it arrived. You find yourself in a large room. It is four-sided, a square. Upon the floor are tiles of white marble and black onyx with a fabulous citrine dragon inlaid upon them. The north is directly in front of you, the south behind, the east to your right, the west to your left. Upon each wall is a brightly illustrated mural depicting various magickal beasts. Turning to the left and the west, you face the image of a magnificent and ferocious white tiger. You realize that this image is painted upon steel doors, studied and cold. They are a dull blue, heavy and imposing.

Your heart beats slowly in your chest, and you are overwhelmed with a sense of peace and well-being. All fears and worries are banished from your mind; you stand tall and alone. The swoosh of blood in your ears is now layered with the whistle of the wind in trees desperately holding on to their summer raiment. A pale gray light seeps from under the door. Take a deep breath and push it open.

The door opens into the mouth of a cave situated on a windswept mountainside. Down the tunnel, you hear the sounds of pickaxes, machinery, and engines. Industry exists in this place; metal strikes metal, and it smells like blood. A young woman in a pale gray coverall walks slowly up through the tunnel. She has a sword at her hip and steel bracers and greaves upon her arms and legs. She is without a doubt a warrior, but you know in your heart she is also more. As she levels with you, she smiles and extends her hand toward you, open-palmed, in a sign of friendship and peace. Her name is Potnia; she is the daughter of Cain.

Turning toward the landscape below, you can see the world laid out before you. Strange luminous lines appear as if to mark out borders. Some areas flicker, as if not entirely in this realm. There is almost a doubling of vision, as if two images are overland, one on top of the other. She whispers to you, "Are you ready for the harvest? Our battle lines are drawn, and I will fight to protect my own." Panicked, you look into her eyes. What does she mean? She has no sclera, and you get lost in her gaze. You see denizens of Faerie fighting a battle against humankind. Some win, and they find a place to be. Some are losing and have no home. Some are so changeless and eternal they have not even realized that humanity exists. Let these scenes play out in her eyes. Take in all she has to share with you. Learn how the spirits of metal may be the link required to make peace with the urban Fae and beyond. Take your time; do not be frightened by the strange images she shows you. She has no desire to harm you. She seeks only allies.

Her eyes start to dull, the sclera returning. A single silver tear trickles down her face, and leaves and twigs skitter around both your feet. The world dissolves, and again you are on the checkerboard floor. When you are ready, call out and ask the mist to carry you home, to the here and now.

FINDING OTHER FAE

With Fae who are associated with the element of metal, the most vital lesson is to remember that not all metals mean iron. It also means being open to the idea that some Fae aren't allergic to iron, or possibly no Fae are actually allergic to iron alone—only when we are holding it. Once you are open to this, you will find it much easier to seek out possible manifestations. Try looking for ghost stories involving metal or treasure. These may well be Fae who have been given another name because of the elemental disconnect.

PECHS—THE BUILDERS OF THE STONE CIRCLES

The pechs were a small dwarfish race responsible for building the many large stone circles and dolmens that litter the highlands of Scotland. It is also said that they knew the secret of brewing heather beer and were responsible for building Glasgow Cathedral. Who these pechs were has been argued left, right, and center. Some academics think they are a memory of the Picts who once ruled the landscape that survived into the modern world, but one wonderful tale tells of a more supernatural origin.

It is said that as the last pech sat fading away, he overheard younger men talking of their feats of strength. Incredulous of their claims, he asked one of the young men to let him feel his wrist so that he could gauge their true strength. As the poor creature was crippled and half blind, the young men thought it would be funny to hand the creature an iron bar, expecting to make a fool of him. As the bar was passed to him, the pech took hold of it with both hands and snapped it like a twig, proclaiming aloud, "It's a bit gey gristle, but nothing to the shackles-banes o' my young days."

I seriously doubt that the pechs are dead. They, just like many Fae, choose to hide themselves a bit better than they once did and also allow us to be blissfully blind in our technological society. But should you happen upon one, consider asking for help with building, creating, or being strong.

BENDITH Y MAMAU—THE MOTHER'S BLESSINGS AND THEIR HOARDS OF GOLD

In at least two regions of Wales, we hear of the Bendith y Mamau, the Mother's blessings. They are generally joyful Fae who are willing to help in return for kind words and milk and honey. They seem to be the rulers of the faery ring, and you should consider leaving them a gift if you choose to work within faery rings (discussed in chapter 6).

Several folktales claim that they resided deep within caves full of gold, and there is some suggestion that they were willing to provide money to those whom they looked favorably upon, as long as that person did not tell of the gifts to other people. If you are short a bob or two, finding a faery ring and asking for some help from these folk may not be a bad idea.

THE CURIOUS CASE OF THE LIVERPOOL LEPRECHAUNS

One of the most curious cases of urban Fae in living memory is that of the Liverpool leprechauns. Leprechauns, with their connections to pots of gold and treasures secreted in caves along with their mercurial, tricksterlike behavior, are another perfect example of Fae who are definitely aligned to the element of metal.

The city of Liverpool has a long history spanning over a thousand years and was a key port during the industrial revolution. As such, in modern times, it is heavily industrialized and urbanized. That the sighted Fae were named leprechauns is also not surprising, for Liverpool is one of the major ferry ports that cross between the UK, Ireland, and the Isle of Man, so Liverpool has a population with a strong Irish ancestry.

In the summer of 1964, a series of events took place that made it to the national newspapers.[47] Children in the Edge Lane area of the city started returning home injured. Superficial cuts and bruises only, but all of them reported that the injuries had occurred because little men in white hats were throwing stones on the bowling green. Thus ensued a summer filled with frantic faery hunts, mass sightings, and even reports that the leprechauns may have traveled from Ireland via some form of faery airplane thanks to several UFO sightings farther up the coastline. There have been a number of people over the years who have claimed to be the originator of the phenomena, but in each case, the inconsistencies in their stories suggest that they were just trying to cash in on their fifteen minutes of fame. Many more have tried to debunk the tale as of course "nonbelievers" would, but it is my opinion that at the core, there was and to this day remains a coterie of Fae who live and operate in the city.

As treasure Fae, it may be worthwhile to call to them when you perform your walking meditations, for they are certainly the Fae who help you find money when you are out walking. Just beware—they may trip you when you bend down to pick it up!

MACHINE ELVES—A FINAL WORD

Some fifteen years after the Liverpool leprechaun event, another mass sighting took place about eighty miles away in the city of Nottingham—again, a heavily industrialized city that was founded on the textile and coal mining industries.[48] During the autumn of 1979, multiple reports by children were recorded by the children's headmaster stating that they had seen little men sitting in pairs

---

47. Nigel Watson, "The Liverpool Leprechauns," Magonia Archive, accessed October 2019, http://magoniamagazine.blogspot.com/2013/11/the-case-of-liverpool-leprechauns.html.

48. Simon Young, "Wollaton Park Gnomes Tape Transcript," Academia, accessed March 30, 2020, https://www.academia.edu/30103864/Wollaton_Park_Gnomes_Tape_Transcript.

driving strange cars. Fae using machinery is often ignored by faery hunters, probably because of the desire to disassociate them with metal, and yet it is well-known among ufologists and enthusiasts of unexplained phenomena, often referred to as forteana, that certain Fae can use technology. They have earned the title of machine elf, which feels very fitting, somehow.

· EXERCISE ·
Graffiti scrying image activity

You may like to use this image to practice elemental graffiti scrying (discussed in chapter 6).

Portal for the Element of Metal—Runcorn, UK
Photographed by Tara Sanchez

water

There's no doubt it's the most versatile of the five elements.
It can wash away earth; it can put out fire; it can wear a piece of metal down
and sweep it away. Even wood, which is its natural complement, can't survive
without being nurtured by water.[49]

Humanity would never have become the advanced race we are today without the advent of fire, discovering how to harness the land, building shelters of wood and stone, and the ability to manipulate various metals. As a species, we have had an ongoing relationship with all the elements (and probably the elementals) since we first crawled out of the primordial soup. But no life at all would have existed without water, the most fundamental of the elements. The Fae who are aligned to water are often extremely powerful and are still very aware of who they are, where they are, and what their purpose is. They also adapt very well to urban environments.

MODERN SIGHTINGS—
THE SPIRIT OF ST. JAMES WELL

St. James Cemetery in Liverpool is situated behind the city cathedral. It sits well below ground level, giving it a strange subterranean feel. The site was once a quarry with a chalybeate spring (heavy in minerals and iron salts). In the late 1800s, it was turned into the city cemetery and continued to serve that function for close to a hundred years. A relatively short space of time for the sheer amount of supernatural activity that has been reported there, which suggests something else may be at play.

49. A. Golden, *Memoirs of a Geisha* (London: Penguin Random House, 1997).

It is an eerie location, and the spring, which is heavily mineralized, is known by locals as both a healing and a bewitched spring. Legends tell that the workers who excavated the spring claimed the water was perfectly drinkable when fresh from the ground, exhibiting great healing properties if used to aid the ill or infirm. However, if removed from the site for storage or boiled, it would turn black and putrid. For many years, this was taken as a sign from the spirit of the spring that they were unhappy with their water being used for mundane purposes. This old legend had fallen into obscurity until just a few years ago when a flurry of unusual sightings sparked public interest.

In 2018, an Australian tourist visiting the gardens photographed a particularly overgrown and unloved area of the site. The location was full of nettles and brambles and not traversable. However, when examining the photo later, the tourist discovered that she had captured the figure of a long-haired and bedraggled woman standing right in the middle of the bramble patch. A woman who the tourist claimed had not been there at the time the photo was taken. Since then, numerous sightings of an other-than-human female wandering the cemetery have come to light, and so it would certainly appear that the spirit of the spring is alive and well and becoming braver, as she has now been seen walking pathways in and around the spring.

In the wu xing, the element of water is associated with the winter season, a time of deep contemplation. Its planetary correspondence is Mercury. It is an element of intuition and psychic development and supernatural activity. And on a more mundane level, its connection with Mercury means that it is also associated with wisdom and mirth in equal measure, as well as communication and diplomacy. Travel overseas and business opportunities involving the arts or creative disciplines all fall into the realm of water.

Water need not be just of the river, stream, and sea variety. Our blood and other mucus secretions are primarily water, and our bodily cycles are affected by the moon, which has a massive effect on us and the world around us. While there are more than a few differences between the Western and Eastern elemental systems, when it comes to esoteric correspondences, water has a lot of similarities. I might even go out on a limb and suggest that most of the world's major philosophies have some kind of elemental theory, and they all, at least to some extent, associate water with spiritual development, emotions, intuition, and magick.

Water is a much-maligned element, in my opinion. If you are someone who feels deeply or expresses your opinion in a heartfelt and passionate manner, you are often described as a bit watery or wishy-washy. And woe betide you if you happen to be a water sign, particularly a Pisces. For some reason, people always talk about them as if they are the poor relatives of the astrological signs. And yet, this couldn't be further from the truth. And when it comes to the Fae associated with the element of water, never will you find a more badass collection of spirits.

Mere-maids, pegs, jennies, selkies, undines, sirens, nymphs, nerids—the list goes on and on. The sheer quantity of documented water spirits is indicative of how fundamental our connection to this element actually is, as it appears that after wood, this is the element in which we have most often witnessed the Fae. The number of sightings that continue into modern times would suggest that this is still the case. These Fae, given the right relationship, may help you develop certain mental and spiritual skills, allow you to divine for and plan a future, and even communicate with others on the subtle levels, influencing a situation in subconscious ways.

While most water spirits can be safely placed within the element of water, there are a few notable exceptions. The lamia whom we met in the element of earth is one such being. Others, such as the Cornish korrigan and the Breton groac'h, are often designated as water spirits, but this is a misclassification. Although all can be found near bodies of water, fountains, springs, fords, and sea caves, they aren't always inherently of the water and are best considered a watery aspect of another element.

CASE STUDY 1: JENNY GREEN-TEETH

My first urban Fae for this chapter is the first Fae whom I knowingly had an ongoing relationship with, and while I didn't feel quite the same fear, she left my companions quite literally quaking in her presence. She is a Jenny Green-teeth, and she lived by the weir at the back of an old mill in a town in Cheshire. The banks are dirty and polluted. Kids light fires on its sandy shores; tires and shopping carts litter the shallows. And that is just the modern pollution in a section of the willow-covered floodplain. I discovered rusting ore carts and evidence of smelting, probably from the early part of the industrial revolution when carts and machinery for the mill would have been fixed on site in a small foundry.

When I first started exploring the site, I was aware that something of the Fae was there. Her energy is very distinct and not entirely welcoming. She can come across as something foreboding and malevolent when she wishes to. So, I had first resolved to keep a respectful distance and hoped that she would do the same—until I came across one of her sisters in Derbyshire in an encounter that I couldn't ignore. That sparked a flame of interest, encouraging me to engage with my local spirit.

The river that runs through this Cheshire town has a little reputation for drownings. In places, it is very fast—during the winter, dangerously so. In my time living there, at least one late-night reveler was last seen close to its banks before disappearing, never to be seen again. Discussing this alarming state of affairs, I asked her one evening if she was responsible. In folklore, those of her kind are often blamed for dragging victims into the depths (usually small boys and handsome young men). She was very put out by this suggestion. Once, this might have been common practice, but no longer. More on that in a moment.

Jenny, if you haven't guessed already, is the third type of feral faery: class 3, fully conscious. She is 100 percent comfortable in our world. I'm not exactly sure she has changed or transitioned in any tangible way other than how she uses the landscape around her. Sometimes she gives me the impression she is so primeval that the growth and development of civilization is something her kind has seen before and will see again; they will just adapt and endure.

Her understanding of her role is very interesting. She believes her relationship with humanity is a deliberately symbiotic one, which may explain her ability to remain so cognizant of the world around her no matter how much it changes. She can wax lyrical about it, too!

I am the moon in the water; I am the illusion of reality.
Man always strives to pursue that which he perceives to be real, not what is.
And when he grasps beyond his reach, he falls into my depths. That is my function,
for if man in unison started reaching for reality, then my mother would cease to exist.
I keep the balance for my mother's sake; I ensure her survival by tempting man with
illusion, and I do it alone.[50]

---

50. From conversations with Jenny Green-teeth.

Anyway, she knows exactly who she is, what she wants, and what she is willing to do for you if you approach her respectfully. And it was because of this complete sentience, this obvious symbiosis to this part of the river, that I asked her if she could do anything to perhaps reduce the number of accidents along the banks. She asked for just two things.

First, that I build her a cairn (a pile of stones with quite an elaborate construction). She asked for it to have lumps of quartz, chili peppers, and, the most bizarre thing, a taxidermy hooded crow, which somehow magickly came into my possession just a short while later.

Second, I was to tell people whenever possible the reason for the cairn and teach them how to use it. Where once her race would drag an unsuspecting victim into the depths and feed upon their energy, they have discovered that humanity has more than enough sadness, dysfunction, and regret to keep her race sustained without them ever needing to take a life. They have observed this for hundreds of years: the unhappy folk who walk along the riverbanks, lost in their thoughts about the departed, a lover who has jilted them, or a child estranged. More than a few of these people pick up stones on their walks and hold them as they unwittingly focus upon their emotions, and they cast that stone, energy and all, into the water.

These water Fae now have a wonderful symbiotic relationship with the human race. They do, quite literally, want to take our pain away. They are very proud of their piles of rocks; they see them as treasure, which probably explains the reason she asked me to build a cairn on the banks. What a coup to get a human to consciously build one for her! That is something to tell her sisters about, that is for sure.

So, anyway, I built her cairn, crow and all, and I started teaching about her way of energy exchange and how Jenny Green-teeth can be bargained with to become a protective spirit. And then something changed. I wasn't sure what, so one day I took myself back to her favorite hangout near the weir to discover her cairn had been destroyed—not a dog just sniffing around in the bushes, disturbing it and knocking a few rocks over; this was full-on wanton destruction, or, should I say, intentional deconstruction. The large crystal geometric shapes I had included were gone, the rocks scattered, the taxidermy crow nowhere to be seen, and she was livid at the people who took it away, people she made quite clear were of my kind, which, after long hours of questioning and meditating, I can only surmise were either Pagans, magicians, or witches, or any combination of those three. It took a lot of offerings of whole chickens to get her to calm down.

· EXERCISE ·
Building a cairn

Some years ago, I came across an interesting reference to something called the stones of Diana. They were found at a fountain in the Ardennes, where the Christian monk Remacle settled and built a monastery. He claimed that he had found evidence of early Pagan practice, including a statue of the goddess Diana and the aforementioned stones.

Although there is little to explain what these stones may be, archaeologists have suggested that these may have been altars of some form. I knew immediately what they were: a collection of beautifully rounded stones collected carefully and built into a cairn to be used as a focal point in worship and magickal workings.

In recent years, it has become fashionable among walkers and visitors to sites of beauty to create stacked stone sculptures, and there has been a lot of discussion as to whether these sculptures are damaging the landscape. In the United States, for example, moving, disturbing, or dislodging rocks is actually against the rules in most national parks. This is because relocating rocks can have a detrimental effect on the microbiological flora in a river, the living and breeding environment of fish and freshwater crustaceans, and even the watercourse, affecting the land-dwelling creatures that make their homes in the surrounding areas.

This embargo on performing this exercise in rural locations has actually made it the perfect exercise to perform at home. A small collection of stones that you have gathered in a bowl of water on an altar or in your garden is the perfect way to connect with Jenny. And if you can collect that water from the banks of the river that runs through your town or city, even better.

You can use this cairn for various things:

• A focal point for meditation

• A scrying bowl

• A place to leave offerings to the water Fae

• Somewhere to petition for help and perform spells by writing wishes on a new stone and placing it upon the cairn

Buying nicely rounded decorative stones from a builder merchant or garden center is absolutely fine when creating your cairn. As is taking your time to just pick up the odd stone here and there over time. It's always about quality over quantity with every Fae I have worked with, and the water Fae are no exception. White quartz can be very decorative and is a readily sourced stone that doesn't require unethical strip-mining. It is also naturally a stone of cleansing and spiritual and psychic regeneration. It is ideal for a cairn, so seriously consider including some quartz in your construction.

ALIGNING YOURSELF WITH WATER

One of the points of the elemental exercises is that, if you can allow yourself to bodily and energetically synchronize with the frequencies of each of the elements, then, paired with the breathing exercises, it is much easier to make an initial contact with the faery realms. The water element in particular is very powerful as we are already aligned, being primarily made of water ourselves. It is almost a certainty that one of the reasons the water Fae seem to have retained their consciousness and have an uncanny ability to adapt is because they are closer to us energetically than any of the other Fae species.

You may like to do the following to increase your connection to water: go swimming, scry into rivers and puddles, dance in the rain, drink more water than normal, take a sacred bath, cry at a really sad film, eat only watery foods (milk-based foods, soups, watermelon), and wear only water-related colors.

· EXERCISE ·
finding the spirit of water

Find something made of water. As we are looking at spirits who now reside more or less comfortably in our world, we aren't looking for water from some ancient spring—unless that spring can be found pouring from a fountain in a busy street. Possible items may be the following:

• Steam from a kettle or saucepan

• Water from a garden rainwater barrel

- Canal water
- Dirty puddle water

As with all the other elements, make sure you pick a time when you aren't going to be disturbed for a while. Start by spending a few minutes working with the verdant breath. Allow the spirit of ivy to cleanse your body and mind, preparing you for the work ahead.

There are certain water types that I would recommend over others. I would suggest you avoid processed fluids, such as distilled, ionized, or bottled water. The processing and storage in plastic bottles really mess with any indwelling spirit. Alcohol is another fluid that should only be considered at a later date. The absinthe faery is most definitely real and amazing when worked with creatively, but it's best left until you understand the essence of water better.

Having a bath was deliberately omitted from the list of suggested water elements to experiment with, for while a bath is a really great way of first connecting with the element of water, it won't give you a sense of all the ways that water can exist. By all means, go ahead and take time in the bath to observe and feel the element, but don't make it your only way of connecting.

When experiencing the spirit of water, it is less tangible than, say, wood, earth, or metal, and water may evoke emotion as much as sensations. However, please consider how the water feels. Does it feel silky or hard running through your fingers? Believe it or not, hard mineral-laden waters feel significantly different and host different kinds of water spirits. Can you feel any energy from it? Does that energy feel human-made? What emotions come to the surface when you experience each form of water? Happiness, sadness, security?

You may find that water, even water found in very human environments, is probably the closest to its nature-based counterpart. The water in the mountain stream may well have once evaporated from an urban reservoir. The wild ocean wave that caught you by surprise and made you squeal with delight may once have seen the inside of a car radiator or saline bag. So, it's worth spending extra time considering this when you perform these exercises. Can you glean a sense of what the water's previous purpose was?

It is unlikely that you will experience the thought-form phenomenon in quite the same way as you might with human-made objects. But I would consider trying to get some holy water from a sacred spring or well, especially one that belongs to a different religious construct, if you can. Be thoughtful and respectful, obviously. The power of belief can be very profound and affect indwelling spirits, also. Record all your thoughts, feelings, and observations in your field journal.

· EXERCISE ·
rocks, pebbles, sand, and water

There is a fabulous story of a professor who takes a jar and fills it with rocks. Once his students agree that there is no more room, he then drops in handfuls of pebbles, which trickle down between the gaps until, once again, he apparently can fit nothing more inside the jar. Then, he adds sand, which trickles down into the even smaller cracks and crevices. For most people, this is the end of the story, and there is a lovely philosophical tale about the importance of taking care of the big things in life, with everything else just being filler.

But the tale can have a dual meaning. It can also be used to demonstrate the nature of water. If you were to slowly add water to the jar, you would find that the water seeps downward through the microscopic spaces, collecting at the bottom of the jar.

We can be likened to that jar, and by practicing the following simple exercise, we can tap into the awesome potential of water. The exercise could be likened to an inverted third eye opening meditation, where, instead of accessing our higher psychic powers, we deliberately activate our chakras in the reverse order, like water trickling down through every cell and part of our being to the atomic level, tuning in with the primal nature of our very existence: water!

You may perform this exercise standing or sitting (either cross-legged or on a chair, depending on your mobility). Take a moment or two to practice the verdant breath exercise before closing your eyes and beginning your countdown.

Keeping your eyes closed, slowly count through the chakras.

- If you can, see the color white and sense your crown chakra.
- If you can, see the color violet and sense your third eye chakra.
- If you can, see the color blue and sense your throat chakra.
- If you can, see the color green and sense your heart chakra.
- If you can, see the color yellow and sense your solar plexus chakra.

- If you can, see the color orange and sense your sacral chakra.
- If you can, see the color red and sense your root chakra.

As you count through each chakra, let your awareness quite literally flow through your body. Let the color of each chakra infuse your whole body and bleed down into the next, as if a wave of liquid energy is washing over you and draining away, allowing all your preconceptions of what is, what was, and what will be to wash away as you sit in the stillness that will settle over you. Stay like this for as long as you like, but try not to fall asleep. Dreams can be a little funky after this exercise. Take seven deep breaths when you are ready to return.

....

CASE STUDY 2:
THE WASHER AT THE FORD

The washer is a spirit who has definitely traveled well and adapted to urban living. Human-made canals, culverts, flood defenses, and spillways are her new haunt. And although her location may have changed from the naturally forming ford, her purpose has remained mostly the same. She is nearly always a class 3 spirit, fully cognizant of her identity and purpose.

Folktales are very clear as to what she does as well; those who came across her are given an omen of their death. But this isn't the entirety of the story. Yes, it is true that if she appears unbidden, it normally doesn't bode well for the person encountering her. This has led to millennia of dire warnings to avoid riverbanks late in the evening, on Samhain night, or when the Wild Hunt rides. But we are not faint-hearted creatures, and it is possible to meet the washer on a far more even keel, defining our own terms—something she is more than willing to do, for she is not just a harbinger but also an oracle, a giver of signs, omens, and truths, and she does like to tell a tale.

The washer has started to appear in modern urban myth, and in Latin America, she is now often called la mala hora (also malora and malorga). She is a fearsome creature who appears at the stroke of midnight in some liminal location to warn of the death of a loved one or, worse still, your own death.

In 1987, one particular washer in Lancashire known as Peg O'Nell came to the public eye after a spate of misfortunes close to a bridge in Clitheroe was documented by a local reporter. They unearthed the eighteenth-century tale of a poor serving girl who many claimed was also a witch drowned at the ford, which once existed where the bridge now stands. The serving girl, now known as Poor Peg, was sent during a particularly foul and windy night by the mistress of the household to collect water. Some say the mistress hated her so because Peg was having an affair with the master of the house; others say it was because Peg was a rude, surly girl. Either way, the last words the mistress ever spoke to her were, "I hope you fall and break your neck," and so Peg did. It is now said that every seven years, Peg will claim the lives of any who come near the old ford.

· MEDITATION ·
Journey to the spirit of water

Allow your perception of the mundane world to slip quietly away. The image of reality dissolves and blows away like the wind; mist swirls around you, gray, green, sickly yellow. It obscures your vision and numbs your senses. This mist hangs dense, forming condensation on your eyelids, in your hair. Plumes of thick breath billow out in front of you. You feel deeply rooted in this place between places. Take a few moments to ensure you have fully immersed your-self in this other space. This is neither here nor there—a staging point to allow you to acclimatize. Breathe normally. There is nothing to fear.

The mist parts, dissipating almost as quickly as it arrived. You find yourself in a large room. It is four-sided, a square. Upon the floor are tiles of white marble and black onyx with a fabulous citrine dragon inlaid upon them. The north is directly in front of you, the south behind, the east to your right, the west to your left. Upon each wall is a brightly illustrated mural depicting vari-ous magickal beasts. Stay where you are, facing the north, and gaze upon the image in front of you, which is a large black serpent twisted and turning and devouring its own tail. You realize that this image is painted upon doors of crystal-clear ice.

Your heart beats slowly in your chest, and you can feel the essence of ages past flowing through your veins, pumping clarity and happiness through you. The swoosh of blood in your ears is now layered with the chilling howl of wind whistling across barren mountaintops. A cool blue light starts emanating from the doors, casting a pale glow across the checkered floor. Take a deep breath and push the door open.

As the doors swing open, you find yourself swept from your feet as ice creeps across the floor almost instantly; you're slipping and sliding down what you at first believe to be a semifrozen waterfall until you slide into a large, dark, round tunnel. Eventually, it brings you out onto the banks of a human-made waterway, a canal. It's nighttime, and the moon is high and full above you, casting silver beams upon the water rippling in front of you. A figure dressed in black steps out of the shadows and beckons you forth. He whispers his name gently to you: "Nevyn." He is no one and no thing, yet you know in your heart that he is all things to all people.

You step toward him, and he holds out a pale hand, lightly touching your forehead. Lights spark as if behind your mundane vision, and the world takes on a different hue, as if two worlds are now overlaid one on top of the other, or maybe as if you are looking through a glass of water. Questions start flashing through your mind unbidden, things that you do not yet have the answer to, and almost as quickly, the images start to flow. Allow them to run through your mind like water runs through the cracks in a pavement. Try to stay with them until there is not even the scrap of an image left.

Eventually, Nevyn places both his hands upon your shoulders, bringing you round from your trance. You find that somehow you are now kneeling, staring deeply into the moonlit water of the canal. Shivering, you rise, plumes of hot breath indicating that the temperature has dropped suddenly. Nevyn smiles at you, but it is becoming harder to see him, as your frozen breath is now creating a swirling mist that keeps thickening until there is nothing but gray. Looking down, you can just make out the checkerboard floor once again. Close your astral eyes. Take a moment; don't rush to return to reality just yet. This place is here to help you. When you are ready, call out and ask the mist to carry you home, to the here and now.

....

FINDING OTHER FAE

Below are other Fae whom you may find in urban locations. Consider these when you come across any particular spirit that strikes you as a water Fae.

THE BANNICK

This rather fabulous Fae is found in Slavic lore. He is the master of the bathhouse. Described as a somewhat lecherous but mostly benign old man, he is short in stature, with white hair and beard. It is said that he smells divine. The bannick was blessed with the skill of prophecy, and people, young women in particular, would line up outside the bathhouse at certain times of the year to gain the bannick's wise words.

With the advent of internal and personal bathrooms, the bannick has moved indoors. Any supernatural activity detected in or around a bathroom—and by that, I mean a room containing a bath or shower rather than just a toilet—is likely to be a bannick. Long, hot, well-scented baths are a great way to ask a bannick for advice. Folklore states that if you ask it a question and its touch is soft and gentle, then the answer is yes. If it's cold and scratchy, then the answer is no. So, close your eyes in the bath, relax, and ask your question to see what you get!

However, the bannick is the epitome of the Fae's need for politeness and protocol. He dislikes untidiness, cursing, and drunkenness (although he likes a tot of vodka as an offering), and sex in the bath is a complete no-no, so think really carefully about cultivating this bathroom Fae if you like any form of intimacy in the bath.

THE BLACK MERE-MAIDEN

Mere-maids are faery creatures who inhabit lakes across the entirety of Northern Europe. Reports of them are particularly dense in Wales and the North of England, but there are cognates across the world. La llorona, or wailing woman, in Mexico is often said to appear on or around lakes and, in certain places, is capable of prophecy. In Germanic lore, the "white woman" is also a lake dweller. In these cases, there is an aspect of human sacrifice, particularly infanticide, which may suggest an earlier belief or practice.

The story of the black mere-maiden in Derbyshire, England, is a particularly interesting variation of the tale, and although not strictly urban, it is worthy of mention, as the lake is in a remote and very desolate location. The idea of prophecy or otherworldly advice is deeply embedded into its mythos, suggesting something much deeper in our psyche regarding inland bodies of water. In the case of the black mere-maiden, if you invoke her on the first full moon after the solstice, she will tell you your future. Cool, huh?

Not sure which direction to take in your life? Worried about something? Need a little prophecy to guide you? Large, human-made reservoirs found on the outskirts of large towns and cities often also have "ghost" tales attached to them, although whether they are truly ghost or Fae will be up to you to discover. However, it is worth taking time to access your local town reservoirs, if you are able.

· EXERCISE ·
Graffiti scrying image activity

You may like to use this image to practice elemental graffiti scrying (discussed in chapter 6).

Portal for the Element of Water—Granada, Spain
Photographed by Tara Sanchez

CHAPTER 13
air

The light Coquettes in Sylphs aloft repair
And sport and flutter in the air,
Know further yet; whoever fair and chaste
Rejects mankind, is by some sylph embrac'd.[51]

There are Fae who are so ethereal, so airy, that their base element of wood, fire, metal, water, or earth is so minute as to be almost negligible. It is these whom I would choose to assign to air in their own right. Some ellyllon in Welsh folklore are, according to the folklorist Wirt Sykes, thought to live in woods and groves. He likens them to small goblins or elves, which would make you assume that these were some kind of creature of wood. And so they are, but they are the breeze that blows through the wood, the spirits who make the leaves dance, the childlike voices in the wood somewhere just behind you that you can't quite make out, and the ominous silence when you turn to look.

Their cousins, the ellylldan, live in remote places, often in lowland marshes, but sometimes on hills and barren places. They are the will-o'-the-wisps—the ignis fatuus, or foolish fire. Gaseous in nature, they flicker and dance, leading the unsuspecting astray. Although at a base level they belong to fire, many also tend more toward being primarily aligned with air.

Their urban cousins now inhabit deserted highways, cold city streets, and housing estates. The corners you turn when walking that take you into a cross-wind, causing you to lose your breath, are a playground for airy spirits such as these, so you shouldn't have any difficulty finding them. You will have realized from your rhythmic walking meditations that the presence of Fae can often be

---

51. A. Pope, "The Rape of the Lock: Canto 1," Poetry Foundation, accessed March 30, 2020,
   https://www.poetryfoundation.org/poems/44906/the-rape-of-the-lock-canto-1.

heralded by whirls of rubbish at your feet. You may have been blocked by buffeting wind, a natural defense mechanism by the Fae themselves: "Don't come down here; it's cold and desolate. Nothing to see, nothing to see. Move along." These are the air spirits on our city streets, playing with our perceptions.

To ensure that you have a full understanding of and a connection with all the elements of the hybrid system, it is necessary to look at the element of air with a view of modern-day sightings and to dedicate some time to inner practices as well. So, despite the fact that there are no Eastern correspondences to give you for this element, what we can do is look at the traditional Western elemental correspondences instead to gain a fuller understanding of the Fae who fall most readily into this elemental category. The occultist Cornelius Agrippa stated in the first of his amazing occult books of philosophy that "the Hebrew Doctors reckon it not amongst the Elements, but count it as a Medium or glue, joyning things together," a validation of the system we have been working with here in our journeys with the Fae.[52] He also goes on to suggest that it is air that communicates with the planets and provides knowledge in dreams and divinations.

These early attributions have led air to be associated with intellect, sciences, communication, and anything that lends itself to cold, hard reasoning and precise analysis. Not always fitting when we consider the air-type Fae we find around us, but if we remember Agrippa's words, it all makes a little bit more sense. In this chapter, I have included a modern sighting from my own hometown and the alignment exercises, but there are no personal case studies, as, ironically, my own experiences with air-type Fae are so brief and intangible, much like the air Fae themselves. The case studies will have to be your own.

MODERN SIGHTINGS— THE RUNCORN THING

Many encounters with the spirits of the otherworld are often miscategorized as hauntings when, in fact, they are without any doubt a manifestation of the faery kind. This is not a new assumption, either. Allan Kardec, the famous spiritualist, believed all poltergeist activity to be very specifically connected to elemental beings.

---

52. H. C. Agrippa, *Three Books of Occult Philosophy* (Woodbury, MN: Llewellyn Publications, 2009).

One such event is that of the Runcorn Thing. On the night of August 10, 1952, seventeen-year-old John Glynn and his grandfather, Sam Jones, made their way to bed in their little two-up, two-down terraced house, the likes of which are found all over the North of England. At that time, the towns of Runcorn and Widnes, which sit on either side of the Mersey Estuary, were thriving hubs of industry known worldwide for tanning factories, salt, and chemical works. The house and the family had never before experienced any kind of supernatural activity, and the house is still inhabited to this day, for no further incidents have ever been reported.

Shortly after the pair had retired, they started hearing scratching and scraping noises emitting from behind a large dresser in the bedroom. The dresser had been in the possession of Old Sam for quite a while—most of his adult life, in fact, and again, nothing untoward had ever been reported in relation to this item of furniture. Believing this noise to be a rodent of some kind, the pair attempted to locate the intruder, but to no avail. During the investigations, the noises stopped, only to restart once both men had returned to their beds. Over a period of nights, the noises and disturbances escalated. Heavy furniture was moved, precious items were smashed, there were constant noises, and eventually physical harm came to anybody who dared to enter the bedroom.

Both Sam and John had to move out, as the situation became unlivable, and a steady stream of spiritualists, paranormal investigators, clergy, and even a few police officers and reporters all attempted to find, debunk, hold séances with, and even exorcise the noisy spirit.

Many of the events had strong similarities to the Zaragoza goblin discussed in chapter 8, with a young person being initially blamed for the outbreak (poor John was readily blamed for the problems). In each story, this theory would be disproved. Where this story deviates is at the point where the family moved out. This tale takes an even more astonishing turn, as numerous corporeal manifestations were reported, including at the farm where Old Sam worked. The owners of Pool Farm were blighted with regular visitations of a dark, cloudlike apparition, which they claimed killed over fifty of their pedigree rare breed pigs and even chased Mr. Crowther, Old Sam's employer, around the kitchen of the farmhouse.

It is reported that these two men decided to visit the haunted bedroom, believing the two incidents to be linked, which they were. When they entered the room together, the apparition appeared, this time so wrathful that it caused plaster to fall from the walls and carpeting to be damaged. The two men ran for their lives. As with the Zaragoza goblin, the manifestations did eventually die out in the latter half of December, never to be heard from again.

One final twist to this story remains. In the early 2000s, a man wrote to a local magazine that had recently run a retro piece about the affair. He claimed to have been a friend of John Glynn at the time, and that both he and John had spent an evening in the property trying to get the spirit to talk to them through a series of raps and knocks. It was not explained exactly how they did this, but apparently the spirit had admitted that his name was JuJu and that he was an African witch doctor! Knowing what we do about the Fae and their names, this suggests a trickster spirit rather than a ghost. This is further evidenced by the change in location of the manifestation, which is highly unusual in hauntings. The nature of the cloud apparition, along with the lack of actual interaction or obvious purpose (remember, even the Zaragoza goblin was prepared to talk to its poor victims), gives it an intensely airy signature. Ghost of a witch doctor, or an air Fae? I know which I believe to be the most plausible.

ALIGNING YOURSELF WITH AIR

While performing these exercises, consider doing the following: take a walk on a windy day, work with your windows open (even if it's cold), watch a windmill, fill your garden with colorful pinwheels, eat only airy foods (candy floss, puff pastry, etc.), and wear only air-related colors.

· EXERCISE ·
finding the spirit of air

The first part of this exercise is to find something made of air. Air doesn't belong as part of the wu xing, but it is part of the Western system. However, as it has been presented to me that the Fae feel more akin to a combination of the two systems, it is necessary to learn to align ourselves with air to understand the full complexity of their natures. As with fire, it will not always be possible to physically touch this element, so near enough is good enough. Possible items may be the following:

- Cool air from a mechanical source (ceiling fan)
- Warm air from a mechanical source (heater)

- Wind in a subway tunnel
- The air from the rush of cars on a busy road

Always pick a time when you aren't going to be disturbed for a while, and start by spending a few minutes working with the verdant breath. Allow the spirit of ivy to cleanse your body and mind, preparing you for the work ahead.

· MEDITATION ·
journey to the spirit of air

Allow your perception of the mundane world to slip quietly away. The image of reality dissolves and blows away like the wind; mist swirls around you, gray, green, sickly yellow. It obscures your vision and numbs your senses. This mist hangs dense, forming condensation on your eyelids, in your hair. Plumes of thick breath billow out in front of you. You feel deeply rooted in this place between places. Take a few moments to ensure you have fully immersed yourself in this other space. This is neither here nor there—a staging point to allow you to acclimatize. Breathe normally. There is nothing to fear.

The mist parts, dissipating almost as quickly as it arrived. You find yourself in a large room. It is four-sided, a square. Upon the floor are tiles of white marble and black onyx with a fabulous citrine dragon inlaid upon them. The north is directly in front of you, the south behind, the east to your right, the west to your left. Upon each wall is a brightly illustrated mural depicting various magickal beasts. Lift your arms skyward and tilt back your head. Directly above you is the image of an eagle in flight. You realize that this image is painted upon billowing silks, which, if you reach just a little higher, you can move out of the way with your hands.

Your heart beats slowly in your chest, and you can feel the knowledge of ages past flowing through your veins, pumping life and wisdom through you. The swoosh of blood in your ears is now layered with the whistling and howling of a stormy night. A pale blue light starts to seep through the silks, flickering and dancing. Take a deep breath, reach up, and part the silks above you. As the silks part, you find yourself swept from your feet by the sheer force of the wind that rushes down from above. Expecting to fall, you are surprised when you never hit the floor. Instead, you rise slowly through the silks onto a windswept city street. A fountain trickles slowly to your left-hand side. It emits a slightly acrid smell, probably from the oily scum floating on the pool's surface—a layer of grime from the vehicles that rumble past day and night.

Beside the fountain is a wooden bench, upon which a small, wizened man sits. His hair is white and wispy, his face birdlike: bright, sparkling eyes full of intelligence and laughter. He smiles and beckons you forward to join him. He says his name is Aderyn, and he is here to show you what you need to know. As you lower yourself down, time seems to shift, moving faster than before, like a time-lapse photograph. Occasionally, the scene will freeze, showing you a glimpse of an image: a businessman on a mobile phone; a student, arms laden down with books; a young mother with her child in tow, shopping bags heavy in each arm, tired and harassed, wondering when the bus will arrive. Take your time here. Immerse yourself in what you see. It may seem like days—maybe even weeks—pass, day and night flickering and blurring into one, but try to take in as much as you can. You will not hunger, you will not thirst, and you will not get cold or old, so never fear.

Eventually, time will start to slow, and Aderyn stands and indicates that it is time for you to go home. You rise to grasp his hand, but yours passes right through, and as it does, the world around you dissolves, bit by bit. The final thing you see is the old man's beaming smile. You find yourself on the checkerboard floor once again. Take a moment; don't rush to return to reality just yet. This place is here to help you. When you are ready, call out and ask the mist to carry you home, to the here and now.

· EXERCISE ·
Graffiti scrying image activity
You may like to use this image to practice elemental graffiti scrying (discussed in chapter 6).

Portal for the Element of Air—Granada, Spain
Photographed by Tara Sanchez

working with the seasons

Singing, singing, through the night,
Dancing, dancing with our might,
Where the moon the moor doth light,
Happy ever we![53]

Like any culture, the Fae have a seasonal cycle. Read through any book of folk-lore and mythology, and you find that magickal events and interactions with the Fae often happen at key points in the year. But just as with humanity, there are regional variations. And not all clusters of appearances or activities have a rhyme or reason, nor are they all linked to an agrarian or lunisolar calendar.

It would be easy to say that the ebb and flow of contact with humanity throughout the seasons is a result of the fair folk being "of" nature, but as they aren't entirely of this world, I suspect that they are as much at the whim of this rock we inhabit and its whimsical nature as we are. For while it looks like they are working magick based on the seasons alone, all it means is that they just know how to access the power inherent in any landscape, urban or otherwise, and they have harnessed it to their advantage. A knowledge that we can also gain with a bit of time, practice, and help from our faery friends.

The wheel of the year is now so ingrained in the modern Pagan worldview that it would be foolish to go against the flow, especially when so many of the key dates fit so nicely within it. However, there are some notable and probably surprising differences in the faery year. Primarily, the equinoxes. We have all been told that these are times of balance, and it is precisely because of this that

---

53. J. Rhys, *Celtic Folklore, Welsh and Manx* (London: Wildwood House, 1980).

little happens at these times. Equinox folklore is very sparse as a result. The Fae revel in imbalance—the times of mischief and discord, the times when balance is no longer achievable.

The Zaragoza goblin incident didn't start until late September after the equinox was well past and darkness had taken hold, growing in force throughout October and November before tailing off in December. He was a creature of the Wild Hunt, of the season of misrule, rather than of some arbitrary date set by humanity. And so it is with many of the tales we hear of the Fae. As a general rule, their behaviors and activities follow a season rather than an astrological festival.

You may find that some of the Fae are more easily contactable at the time of year associated with their element, so please take note of this as you read on.

TROOPING DAYS

Possibly the closest thing to faery festivals that exist are what I've called trooping days. It is these trooping days that probably led to the concept of the seelie and unseelie courts in Scotland, for they are the major shifts between the time of the Wild Hunt and the time of the faery queens. These two main trooping days roughly align with Beltane and Samhain, which we shall look at in more detail later. However, you will find that there are other localized events. A quick search for local myths and legends online or in books written by local historians and folklorists will often help reveal these events. But even if you don't turn something up through academic research, it's likely that using your instinct will allow you to start tapping into these times. The key is to remember that these dates may not occur on exactly the same date each year.

· EXERCISE ·
look for patterns

In my experience, metrological conditions are often the trigger for Fae-related events. It's common for there to be an unusually warm weekend in spring and a day in autumn when the light changes and you feel chilled to the bone for the first time. If you examine your journal or even check social media accounts that allow you to look back on "this day" in previous years, it's surprisingly easy to see the patterns that may give you clues for these shifts. The patterns may be as simple as an innocent note that the dog was skittish when you were walking through a local park or down a particular path that's not normally a problem. By looking back, you can see that, give or take a few days, you have reported the same thing several years running. Try it, I urge you. It's alarmingly insightful for many reasons.

· EXERCISE ·
visit faery portals

Most trooping activity happens in or around the faery portals, rings, thorn gates, and so on in heavily urbanized areas. These may well be the graffiti points, as we have previously discussed. But many will also be found in places where natural gateways occur. Bridges, subways, spillways, and alleys are all viable places for this activity. In Scotland, there is a famous bridge that, for the last fifty years, has been the site of over fifty recorded suicides. These aren't any normal suicides, either, for the poor souls taking their lives are primarily canine. For no apparent reason, these poor pooches become agitated and launch themselves to their almost certain death. It has even been reported that the few dogs who survived their fall onto the rocks below were drawn to return and repeat their actions, thus removing the question of it just being a statistically abnormal "accident" spot. Many mundane explanations have been given for this bizarre behavior, but without a shadow of a doubt, the bridge is close to a faery portal, for many have reported strange feelings and faery activity in the area.

Obviously, I urge utmost caution. If you are going to a city park or piece of undeveloped land near an industrial area after dark, then please take someone with you. Or at the very least let people know where you are going and when you intend to return. Use your instinct as well; so often I hear people say that they had a bad feeling about a place or situation, and yet they chose to ignore it to their eventual peril. The gift of fear is essentially one of humanity's greatest abilities. The world isn't going to end if you decide that it's just too darn spooky to go investigating a phenomenon that particular night. Heed your feelings; you are probably picking up on something important.

THE TIME OF THE FAERY QUEENS AND THE WILD HUNT

IMBOLC

In Scotland, it's fair to say that Imbolc is pretty important. There are hundreds of variations of the tale of the goddess Brigit complete with the Faery Prince Angus riding out to win her heart, steal her away from the crone of winter, and gift her with a magickal crystal that sits above her heart, shining like a star. In the Irish version of her myth, the young girl who was to become St. Bride was fed the milk of a faery cow. Each night, her Druid father would venture deep into the woods, where a white-haired, red-eared cow would allow him to draw two pails full of milk and then disappear until sundown the following evening. The milk is what gave her great wisdom and her devout spiritual nature.

You can use this time to make offerings to the goddess, her faery prince, and even the faery cow, if you wish. Petitions to aid your spiritual growth, enhance your love life, and be provided for in the coming year can and should be left at portal sites or on a home altar or in a constructed faery ring ritual.

SPRING EQUINOX

Most wood-type Fae are best contacted in the weeks surrounding the spring equinox. The sap in many of the trees has risen, energy is at its best before the first push of new growth begins, and buds burst forth with leaves. This is the case whether you are in the town or the country; in fact, spring is likely to be earlier in a town, because much of the life cycle of trees is dependent on ambient temperature, and thanks to the concrete jungle, temperatures are often just a degree or two warmer in urban environments.

BELTANE

There seems to be a point in the year when there is a natural crossover in energetic power in the world of the Fae. The sensation starts in early April, normally a couple of weeks after the equinox; the blackthorn has almost finished flowering, but a few tenacious bushes still flower, and the hawthorn is tentatively starting to show a few of its heady flowers. Over the coming month, you sense a richer, warmer feeling in the air. When you step out onto the street after a day at work, the light feels more golden, the birds start to sing louder, and you suddenly notice that you don't need a coat. To the unobservant, the day might not be that different from the one before. But you are suddenly struck with awe at the change in energy. That will be a trooping night. At Beltane, the Wild Hunt will pass through the faery portals, and the court of the faery queens will take its place on the edges of our reality. Now is a good time to start monitoring your faery portals.

SUMMER SOLSTICE/MIDSUMMER

Not unsurprisingly, the fire-, earth-, and metal-type Fae are more readily contactable in the weeks before and after the summer solstice. The days are now consistently warm, and with early heat waves now being commonplace thanks to global warming, summer is well underway.

A particular species of Welsh Fae was renowned for invading entire towns and villages during the solstice celebrations, dancing, singing, and carousing through the streets. While the Bendith y Mamau (the Mother's blessings) were mostly harmless if left alone to revel in the streets until dawn, caution was always urged in the older tales to lock doors and windows during this time, ensuring all children were secure on trooping nights. These particular Fae were not above stealing children and leaving changelings in their place. Unsuspecting travelers and farmworkers were also at risk; they were sometimes caught out late at night and swept away with the revels.

What is interesting is that, if you have ever taken the time to walk city streets on a hot summer evening after the sun goes down, the atmosphere of the city will sometimes change very abruptly for no obvious reason. It's not just the usual combination of office workers, summer heat, and alcohol, either. An area will become frenetic; a bar usually quite calm and classy will suddenly be boisterous. Normally, sensible people will throw caution to the wind and stay for just one more drink, despite knowing they have to work tomorrow. When they shake their heads in the cold light of dawn, they will not be able to tell you why they did it, and inexplicable bruises may be on extremities. A lasting reminder that they were pinched by the vodka pixies.

LAMMAS

The earth- and metal-type Fae come into their own at this time of year. As the late August heat hums in the air, the Bendith y Mamau still dance their merry revels, but the mornings promise the start of autumn. The Puck Fair in Ireland is named after one of the most famous trickster and mercurial Fae we know, and it is held during Lammastide.

SAMHAIN

Across the northern hills and coastline of Wales, running into Cheshire and Lancashire, Samhain is a time when the local lore of my area states that the faery folk ride out, led by Faery King Gwyn ap Nudd. However, this isn't just specific to where I live. All across the northern hemisphere, this is the time when the Wild Hunt rules over the land, taking control back from the faery queens. I love Samhain; it's possibly one of the most important festivals of the year for me. Once you start working with this season, you can genuinely feel the magick in the air. When the shift starts, the light takes on an eerie quality long before dusk. Your skin prickles on the back of your neck. You can almost smell the feral musk of the creatures of the hunt slowly waking from their summer slumber. Leaves skitter along in front of you. It's difficult to shake the feeling that something is treading silently just a few steps behind. Whispered voices travel on the wind, and you can almost hear small, scampering feet. There is a pregnant pause—the world holding its breath, waiting for the moment when the final shift happens. Then, faery hounds bray, and the hunt rides forth—ready to sweep any unsuspecting human with eyes to see along—helter-skelter into the long, dark, windswept nights of the winter months ahead.

Water Fae can be particularly sensitive during this time of year, particularly the jennies, pegs, and mere-maidens. The turning to the dark half of the year is, after all, a time of deep contemplation and intuition, so it's not surprising that we should sense these loathly ladies a little more strongly during this time.

WINTER SOLSTICE/MIDWINTER

Jack Frost is an interesting Yuletide Fae. He is the essence of frozen water. He almost certainly rides with the Wild Hunt on the stormiest of nights, bringing blizzard and hail. However, more friendly Fae may be connected with during this time, for although the ground may be frozen above, life will be stirring below. In Norse folklore, the nisse and the tomte are honored around Yule, so we see the introduction of the wood faery back into our calendar year. During this season of goodwill, the domestic helper spirits are given extra offerings, and it is expected that they will take time off from their labors to make merry. In Norwegian lore, it was customary to lay a banquet on Christmas night for the dwarfs to enjoy. Scottish trows don't wait to be given a banquet, preferring to take anything that catches their eye during the holiday period, particularly beer, so you may wish to give your house Fae the night off and leave a little tipple, just to be sure that no mischief is had.

Not all Yuletide Fae are ones you would want to meet, however. The krampus, a pucklike creature with a less-than-sunny disposition, is prevalent in folklore of the season. He punishes small children for behaving poorly. The Yule Lads, seen in the reboot *The Chilling Adventures of Sabrina*, are really a thing. Like the krampus, they will punish naughty boys and girls by leaving a potato in their shoe or stocking rather than a gift. One of the many ways of deterring this kind of behavior was to leave a light or fire burning so that these Fae couldn't enter the home. This makes a silent night vigil by candle or firelight a very apt practice for the season.

OTHER TEMPORAL PHENOMENA
DAWN AND DUSK, FULL AND DARK MOON, MIDDAY AND MIDNIGHT

The time of day in which you approach the Fae is just as important as the time of year. It is a common misconception that the Fae exist only as creatures of the night. And while there are many tales and sightings that do occur in the nighttime hours, there are many tales that refer to daytime contact.

Many modern sightings or experiences are during daylight. The Liverpool leprechauns, the spirit of the well in St. James Cemetery, the Zaragoza goblin, and the Nottingham gnomes were all witnessed during daylight hours. And if you research historical accounts of cunning folk and other workers of charms and magick, you will discover that, while midnight is indeed a very auspicious time to call to the Fae for aid, so, too, are midday, 3:00 p.m., and 6:00 p.m. There are copious accounts of faery doors, portals, pipes, and other phenomena happening at midday at various sites around the UK and beyond. I have personally found that most Fae seem more willing to make a physical appearance just before dawn and after dusk.

These timings seem universal with troops, helper spirits, and other beings in documented lore. In my opinion, there is something about the twilight times that changes how we as humans process sensory information, making us more aware of visual and auditory anomalies and shifts in energy. Basically, in my opinion, we find it easier to see spirits during these times, and my own experiences corroborate this.

Lunar phases also play an important part in the success one has in contacting the Fae. Many reports happen when the moon is full. The Bendith y Mamau are renowned for wreaking havoc in several towns and villages in North Wales during the summer months when the moon is full. And they aren't the only ones. As we have previously discussed, tales state that if you run around a mushroom or faery circle nine times during a full moon, a faery will appear. I have heard it reported as a new moon activity, too, but as it's not so common to find faery circles in urban environments that are secluded enough for me to try this without the neighbors wanting to call the authorities, I haven't tried this yet. Perhaps you can?

I have several theories about moon cycles, though. First, as street lighting is a relatively modern invention, in times gone by, it would have been more likely that people only ventured outdoors during the nights when the moon was at her fullest. Therefore, reports of unusual activity would have centered around these times.

Second, even now we are more likely to want to walk home from a neighbor's or a night out when the moon is full. It has a similar light level to dawn and dusk, allowing us to see more, so I am not entirely sure that the moon itself has that much to do with it—it just allows us to achieve that liminal twilight vision. That being said, there are considerable amounts of Italian folklore that link various sprites, goblins, and pixies with the goddess Diana, a well-known goddess of the moon. So, I am not prepared to say that the light is the only thing that is governing these sightings.

A FINAL WORD

As you work with the Fae in your area, urban or otherwise, you will naturally become attuned to the energies, their shifts, and their cycles. For example, I wake almost nightly at 3:00 a.m. regardless of how much or how little sleep I've had and what time of year it is. This is a time when the Fae in my vicinity are most active, so I will often get out of bed to just acknowledge them and sometimes sit with them in my garden, if the weather is good enough. There is no lore that has taught me this—just instinct. In the latter half of the year, on a wild night when I sense the Wild Hunt is near, I may double-check that all my doors, windows, and energetic boundaries are properly secure before retiring to bed. This is the equivalent of putting an extra log on the fire to stop the hunt from rushing down the chimney. At Beltane, I no longer follow the folklore that states you need to bring hawthorn flowers through your home in a rite of protection against unwanted Fae; instead, a sprig is placed under my front doormat, where it stays for the entire year. After all, I have Fae in my house whom I want to keep there. The sprig is a reminder to any visitors that I know they are there, and an invite is needed to enter. Never harms anyone.

Although I rely heavily on folklore and mythology, I hope you can see through the personal case studies I have provided that pure gut instinct is the most important tool you can have. It was a massive step for me to lay my personal practice open to scrutiny and share experiences, both my own and those of friends and colleagues. But the story of the urban Fae was crying to be told. This book has merely scraped the surface of the work that is left to do so that we can understand the good folk, how they fit into our modern world, and what we can learn about and from them. Hopefully *Urban Faery Magick* will spark an interest that will start you on a lifetime journey of joy, inspiration, and magick.

I wish you love, peace, and joy, and may your brownies never, ever become boggarts!

recommended reading

Bone, Gavin, and Janet Farrar. *Lifting the Veil: A Witches' Guide to Trance-Prophesy, Drawing Down the Moon, and Ecstatic Ritual*. Portland, OR: Marion Street Press, 2015.

Bord, Janet. *Fairies: Real Encounters with Little People*. London: Michael O'Mara Books, 2000.

Carding, Emily. *Faery Craft: Weaving Connections with the Enchanted Realm*. Woodbury, MN: Llewellyn Publications, 2012.

Dukes, Ramsey. *How to See Fairies: Discover Your Psychic Powers in Six Weeks*. London: Aeon Books, 2011.

Evans-Wentz, W. Y. *The Fairy-Faith in Celtic Countries*. London: HardPress Publishing, 2016.

Farhi, Donna. *The Breathing Book: Good Health and Vitality Through Essential Breath Work*. New York: Henry Holt and Company, 1996.

Frantzis, Bruce. *Relaxing into Your Being: The Water Method of Taoist Meditation*. Berkeley, CA: North Atlantic Books, 2001.

Johnson, Marjorie T. *Seeing Fairies: From the Lost Archives of the Fairy Investigation Society, Authentic Reports of Fairies in Modern Times*. Lexington, OK: Anomalist Books, 2014.

Mitchell, Damo. *Daoist Nei Gong: The Philosophical Art of Change*. London: Singing Dragon, 2011.

Palin, Poppy. *Spiritwalking: The Definitive Guide to Living and Working with the Unseen*. Winchester, UK: O Books, 2017.

Vallee, Jacques. *Passport to Magonia: From Folklore to Flying Saucers*. London: Daily Grail Publishing, 2014.

Yang, Jwing-Ming. *Qigong Meditation: Embryonic Breathing*. Boston: YMAA Publications, 2003.

selected bibliography

BOOKS

Agrippa, H. C. *Three Books of Occult Philosophy*. Woodbury, MN: Llewellyn Publications, 2009.

Bacon, F. *The Works of Lord Bacon*. Charleston, SC: Nabu Press, 2011.

Breverton, T. *The Physicians of Myddfai: Cures and Remedies of the Mediaeval World*. Carmarthenshire, UK: Cambria Books, 2012.

Briggs, K. *A Dictionary of Fairies: Hobgoblins, Brownies, Bogies and Other Supernatural Creatures*. Middlesex, UK: Penguin Books, 1977.

———. *The Fairies in Tradition and Literature*. Abingdon, UK: Routledge Classics, 2002.

Burchell, S. *Phantom Black Dogs in Latin America*. Leicestershire, UK: Heart of Albion Press, 2007.

Cabot, L. *Power of the Witch: The Earth, the Moon, and the Magical Path to Enlightenment*. St. Ives, UK: Penguin Books, 1992.

Canard, J. *Defences Against the Witches' Craft: Anti-Cursing Charms from English Folk Magick, Traditional Witchcraft and the Grimoire Traditions*. London: Avalonia Books, 2008.

Chaucer, G. *The Canterbury Tales*. London: Penguin Classics, 2015.

Cooper, L. *The Element Encyclopedia of Fairies: An A-Z of Fairies, Pixies, and Other Fantastical Creatures*. Falkirk, Scotland: Harper Element, 2014.

Curtin, J. *Myths and Folk Tales of Ireland*. New York: Dover Publications, 1975.

Cutchin, J. *A Trojan Feast: The Food and Drink Offerings of Aliens, Faeries, and Sasquatch*. San Antonio, TX: Anomalist Books, 2015.

Fries, J. *Dragon Bones: Ritual, Myth and Oracle in Shang Period China*. London: Avalonia Books, 2013.

Froud, B. *Good Faeries/Bad Faeries*. London: Pavilion Books, 1998.

Froud, B., and A. Lee. *Faeries*. New York: Harry N. Abrams, 1978.

Gaiman, N., and C. Vess. *Instructions*. London: Bloomsbury Publishing, 2010.

Golden, A. *Memoirs of a Geisha*. London: Penguin Random House, 1997.

Harland, J., and T. Wilkinson. *Lancashire Folk-lore Illustrative of the Superstitious Beliefs and Practices, Local Customs and Usages of the People of the County Palatine*. London: Frederick Warne & Co., 1867.

Harms, D., J. R. Clark, and J. H. Peterson. *The Book of Oberon: A Sourcebook of Elizabethan Magic*. Woodbury, MN: Llewellyn Publications, 2016.

Jackson, N. *The Call of the Horned Piper*. Berkshire, UK: Capall Bann Publishing, 1994.

Jacobs, J. *English Fairy Tales*. Overland Park, KS: Digireads, 2011.

Kirk, R., and A. Lang. *The Secret Commonwealth: Of Elves, Fauns, and Fairies*. Glastonbury, UK: The Lost Library, 1893.

Lecouteux, C. *Dictionary of Ancient Magic Words and Spells: From Abraxas to Zoar*. Rochester, VT: Inner Traditions, 2015.

Leland, C. G. *Aradia: Gospel of the Witches*. Newport, RI: The Witches' Almanac, 2010.

Lindahl, C., J. McNamara, and J. Lindow. *Medieval Folklore: A Guide to Myths, Legends, Tales, Beliefs, and Customs*. New York: Oxford University Press, 2002.

Monroe, R. A. *Journeys Out of the Body*. New York: Harmony Books, 2001.

Morehouse, D. *Psychic Warrior: The True Story of America's Foremost Psychic Spy and the Cover-Up of the CIA's Top-Secret Stargate Program*. London: Clairview Publishing, 2004.

Morgan, A. *Toads and Toadstools: The Natural History, Mythology and Cultural Oddities of This Strange Association*. Berkley, CA: Celestial Arts, 1995.

Mullis, D. *West Country Faerie: How and Where to See Nature Spirits*. Cornwall, UK: Bossiney Books, 2006.

Northall, G. F. *English Folk Rhymes 1892*. India: Vjj Publishing, 2019.

Ogden, D. *Magic, Witchcraft and Ghosts in the Greek and Roman Worlds: A Sourcebook*. 2nd ed. New York: Oxford University Press, 2009.

Paine, S. *Amulets: A World of Secret Powers, Charms and Magic*. New York: Thames & Hudson, 2004.

Percy, T. *Reliques of Ancient English Poetry*. London: Edward Moxon, 1844.

Pinch, G. *Magic in Ancient Egypt*. London: British Museum Press, 2006.

Rankine, D. *The Grimoire of Arthur Gauntlet: A 17th Century London Cunning-man's Book of Charms, Conjurations and Prayers*. London: Avalonia Books, 2011.

Rhys, J. *Celtic Folklore, Welsh and Manx*. London: Wildwood House, 1980.

Rowling, J. K. *Harry Potter and the Chamber of Secrets*. London: Bloomsbury Publishing, 1998.

Scott, W. *The Poetical Works of Walter Scott*. London: Houlston and Stoneman, 1848.

Sigerest, H., ed. *Four Treatises of Theophrastus Von Hohenheim Called Paracelsus*. Baltimore: Johns Hopkins University Press, 1996.

Sikes, W. *British Goblins: Welsh Folklore, Fairy Mythology, Legends and Traditions*. US: Sandycroft Publishing, 2017.

Trubshaw, B. *Explore Phantom Black Dogs*. UK: Heart of Albion Press, 2005.

Wen, B. *The Tao of Craft: Fu Talismans and Casting Sigils in the Eastern Esoteric Tradition*. Berkeley, CA: North Atlantic Books, 2016.

Wilby, E. *Cunning-Folk and Familiar Spirits: Shamanistic Visionary Traditions in Early Modern British Witchcraft and Magic*. Brighton, UK: Sussex Academic Press, 2005.

Woods, F. *Further Legends and Traditions of Cheshire*. Nantwich, UK: Shiva Publishing, 1982.

Yeats, W. B. *Fairy and Folk Tales of the Irish Peasantry*. London: Walter Scott, 1888.

Young, S., and C. Houlbrook. *Magical Folk: British and Irish Fairies 500 AD to the Present*. Croydon, UK: Gibson Square, 2018.

WEB REFERENCES

Auden, W. H., and P. B. Taylor. "Hávamál." Wayback Machine. Accessed October 30, 2019. https://web.archive.org/web/20050912100548/http://vta.gamall-steinn.org/havamal.htm.

Bostock, J., and H. T. Riley, eds. "Pliny the Elder, The Natural History." Perseus. Accessed November 10, 2019. http://www.perseus.tufts.edu/hopper/text?doc=Plin.+Nat.+toc.

Briggs, K. "Some Seventeenth-Century Books of Magic." JSTOR. Accessed November 20, 2019. https://www.jstor.org/stable/1257871?origin=JSTOR -pdf&seq=1.

Empedocles. "On Nature." Stanford Encyclopedia of Philosophy. Accessed October 31, 2019. https://plato.stanford.edu/entries/empedocles/#Natu.

Grundhauser, E. "Unconscious Ventriloquism: The Unsolved Mystery of the Zaragoza Goblin." Atlas Obscura. Accessed September 30, 2019. https://www.atlasobscura.com/articles/unconscious-ventriloquism-the -unsolved-mystery-of-the-zaragoza-goblin.

Gyrus. "Verbeia: The Goddess of Wharfedale." Dreamflesh. Accessed November 21, 2019. https://dreamflesh.com/projects/verbeia/.

Hares, G. "A run in with the Fairy (my terrifying experience) AMAZING STORY." YouTube. Accessed October 30, 2019. https://www.youtube .com/watch?v=-BmM57PbdYA&t=12s.

History Disclosure Team. "Duende de Zaragoza: The Case of a Talking Entity." History Disclosure. Accessed October 30, 2019. https://www .historydisclosure.com/duende-de-zaragoza-case-talking-entity/.

Littlejohn, R. "Wuxing (Wu-hsing)." Internet Encyclopedia of Philosophy. Accessed October 31, 2019. https://iep.utm.edu/wuxing/.

Monroe, R. "Our Purpose." The Monroe Institute. Accessed October 31, 2019. https://www.monroeinstitute.org/pages/our-purpose.

Oxford Reference. "Joan the Wad." Oxford Reference. Accessed November 21, 2019. https://www.oxfordreference.com/view/10.1093/oi/authority .20110803100021143.

Pope, A. "The Rape of the Lock: Canto 1." Poetry Foundation. Accessed March 30, 2020. https://www.poetryfoundation.org/poems/44906/the -rape-of-the-lock-canto-1.

Psudowolf. "Master of the Bathhouse: Bannick." The Bestiary. Accessed October 31, 2019. https://shadowsflyte.wordpress.com/2014/05/18/master-of -the-bathhouse-bannick/.

Simon, B. "Five Ages of Man (by Hesiod)." Greek Gods. Accessed October 30, 2019. https://www.greek-gods.org/mythology/five-ages-of-man.php.

Spencer, R. "Peg O'Nell's Well, Waddow Hall, Near Waddington, Lancashire." The Journal of Antiquities. Accessed November 10, 2019. https://the journalofantiquities.com/2018/09/14/peg-onells-well-waddow-hall-near -waddington-lancashire/.

Sussex Archeology & Folklore. "Fairy Folklore." Sussex Archeology & Folk- lore. Accessed November 10, 2019. http://www.sussexarch.org.uk/saaf /fairies.html.

Swancer, B. "Strange Encounters with the Mysterious Little People of… Detroit?" Mysterious Universe. Accessed October 30, 2019. https://myster iousuniverse.org/2017/12/strange-encounters-with-the-mysterious-little -people-of-detroit/.

University of Virginia. "The Chunqiu; with the Zuo Zhuan." Traditions of Exemplary Women. Accessed October 31, 2019. http://www2.iath.virginia .edu/saxon/servlet/SaxonServlet?source=xwomen/texts/chunqiu.xml &style=xwomen/xsl/dynaxml.xsl&chunk.id=d2.16&toc.depth=1&toc .id=0&doc.lang=bilingual.

Young, S. "Wollaton Park Gnomes Tape Transcript." Academia. Accessed March 30, 2020. https://www.academia.edu/30103864/Wollaton_Park _Gnomes_Tape_Transcript.

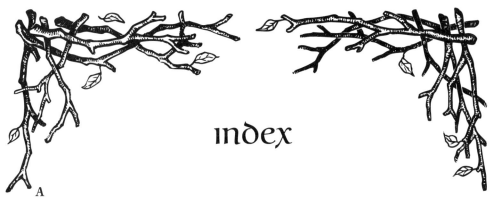

index

TO WRITE TO THE AUTHOR

If you wish to contact the author or would like more information about this book, please write to the author in care of Llewellyn Worldwide Ltd. and we will forward your request. Both the author and the publisher appreciate hearing from you and learning of your enjoyment of this book and how it has helped you. Llewellyn Worldwide Ltd. cannot guarantee that every letter written to the author can be answered, but all will be forwarded. Please write to:

Tara Sanchez
℅ Llewellyn Worldwide
2143 Wooddale Drive
Woodbury, MN 55125-2989

Please enclose a self-addressed stamped envelope for reply,
or $1.00 to cover costs. If outside the U.S.A., enclose
an international postal reply coupon.

Many of Llewellyn's authors have websites with additional
information and resources. For more information,
please visit our website at http://www.llewellyn.com.